D1394293

Oasis

the Gospel to the Poor

JOHN WIMBER

WORD BOOKS
Nelson Word Ltd
Milton Keynes, England
WORD AUSTRALIA
Kilsyth, Victoria, Australia
WORD COMMUNICATIONS LTD
Vancouver, B.C., Canada
STRUIK CHRISTIAN BOOKS (PTY) LTD
Maitland, South Africa
CHRISTIAN MARKETING NEW ZEALAND LTD
Havelock North, New Zealand
JENSCO LTD
Hong Kong
JOINT DISTRIBUTORS SINGAPORE –
ALBY COMMERCIAL ENTERPRISES PTE LTD
and
CAMPUS CRUSADE
SALVATION BOOK CENTRE
Malaysia

© Frontier Publishing International Ltd. 1994

All rights reserved. No part of this publication may be reproduced or transmitted in any form or by any means, electronic or mechanical, including photocopy, recording, or any information storage or retrieval system, without permission in writing from the publisher.

ISBN 0-85009-808-4 (Australia 1-86258-325-0)

Unless otherwise indicated, Scripture quotations are from the New International Version (NIV), © 1973, 1978, 1984 by International Bible Society.
Other Scripture quotations are from the following sources:
The New American Standard Bible (NASB), © 1960, 1962, 1963, 1968, 1971, 1972, 1973, 1975, 1977 the Lockman Foundation.

The quotations in the following studies are all used by permission.

Study 1 from *Bias to the Poor*, by David Sheppard, © 1983. Hodder & Stoughton Ltd., Mill Road, Dunton Green, Sevenoaks, Kent.
Studies 2, 8 from *The Church Unleashed*, by Frank R. Tillapaugh, © 1982. Regal Books, Ventura, CA 93003.
Study 3 from *Why Settle for More and Miss the Best?* by Tom Sine, © Tom Sine 1987. Nelson Word Ltd.
Study 4 from *Can you Hear the Heartbeat?* by Dave Andrews and David Engwicht, © 1989 Dave Andrews and David Engwicht. Hodder & Stoughton Ltd.
Study 5 from *The Positive Kingdom*, by Colin Urquhart, © Colin Urquhart 1985. Hodder & Stoughton Ltd.
Study 6 from *Nine Worlds to Win*, by Floyd McClung Jr. and Kalafi Moala, © Floyd McClung Jr. and Kalafi Moala 1989. Nelson Word Ltd.
Studies 7, 9 from *Issues Facing Christians Today*, by John Stott, © 1984 John Stott. Marshall Pickering an imprint of HarperCollinsPublishers Ltd.
Studies 10, 22 from *The Mustard Seed Conspiracy*, by Tom Sine, © 1981 Word Inc. Marc Europe.
Studies 11, 28 from *Money, Sex and Power*, by Richard J. Foster, © Richard J. Foster 1985. Hodder & Stoughton Ltd./USA and Philippines, Edward England Books.
Study 12 from *Improving Your Serve*, by Charles Swindoll, © 1981. Hodder & Stoughton Ltd./USA and Philippines, Word Inc.
Study 13 from *The Upside-Down Kingdom*, by Donald B. Kraybill, © 1978. Herald Press.
Studies 14, 17 from *The Gift of Giving*, by R.T. Kendall, © 1982 by R.T. Kendall. Hodder & Stoughton Ltd.
Study 15 from *Rich Christians in an Age of Hunger*, by Ronald Sider, © Ronald Sider. Hodder & Stoughton Ltd.
Study 16 from *Radical Discipleship*, by Christopher Sugden, © Christopher Sugden 1981. Marshall Pickering an imprint of HarperCollinsPublishers Ltd.
Studies 18, 23, 31 from *The Call to Conversion*, by Jim Wallis, © Sojourners 1981. Lion Publishing.
Study 19 from *How to Make the World Less Hungry*, by Kathy Keay, © Kathy Keay 1990. Frameworks an imprint of IVP.
Study 21 from *Strength for the Day: Daily Meditations with F. B. Meyer*, compiled by Al Bryant, © 1979 by Word Inc. Nelson Word Ltd.
Study 24 from *Power Evangelism*, by John Wimber, © John Wimber and Kevin Springer 1985. Hodder & Stoughton Ltd./ USA and Philippines, HarperCollinsPublishers Inc.
Study 25 from *Evangelism and the Sovereignty of God*, by J. I. Packer, © J. I. Packer 1961. IVP.
Study 26 from *The Imitation of Christ*, by Thomas à Kempis, translated by Leo Sherley-Price (Penguin Classics, 1952), translation copyright © Leo Sherley-Price 1952.
Study 27 from *Celebration of Discipline*, by Richard J. Foster, © Richard J. Foster 1978. Hodder & Stoughton Ltd./USA and Philippines, HarperCollinsPublishers Inc.
Study 29 from *In Christ Jesus*, by Colin Urquhart, © Colin Urquhart 1981. Hodder & Stoughton Ltd./USA and Philippines, Edward England Books.
Study 30 from *50 Ways You Can Feed a Hungry World*, by Gordon Aeschliman and Tony Campolo © 1991. Kingsway Publications Ltd./USA and Philippines, IVP Publishers, PO Box 1400, Downers Grove, Illinois 60515, USA.

Created, designed and typeset by Frontier Publishing International Ltd., BN43 6RE, England. *Reproduced, printed and bound in Great Britain for* Nelson Word Ltd. *by* Bushey Mead Press, Hailsham.

94 95 96 97 / 10 9 8 7 6 5 4 3 2 1

Making the most of the studies ...

Welcome to the Oasis study on *The Gospel to the Poor*! This book will help you to understand God's compassion for those who tend to be overlooked by society. It will also challenge you to roll up your sleeves and become involved in helping them.

We suggest that you take two days to cover each study and therefore two months to complete the book. You might want to work through the material more quickly, but if you take your time you are likely to benefit more. We recommend that you use the New International Version of the Bible (post-1983 version). The important thing is not that you finish fast, but that you hear from God *en route*! So aim to learn well and steadily build the teaching into your life.

Jesus said, 'Whatever you did for one of the least of these brothers of mine, you did for me' (Matt. 25:40). If we're keen to see Jesus establish His Kingdom among us we must, like Him, identify with the poor and be involved in reaching out to them.

'The church isn't an institution but an organism,' says John Wimber. He challenges the selfish and materialistic outlook of many Christians and exhorts us to give ourselves in humble service to others.

He explains that the Kingdom of God is advanced when we pray for the needy; preach the gospel to them; meet their physical needs; secure justice for them and help them to become integrated into society. He also reminds us that God promises to bless all who remember the poor.

The three sections under the main text relate to the teaching material. You may be asked to consider some aspect concerning the poor, to write down an answer, or to do something practical. The questions and Scripture verses have been designed to encourage you to become more committed to the poor.

The Bible says, 'Wise men store up knowledge' (Prov. 10:14), and Jesus underlines this when He calls us to '[bring] good things out of the good stored up in [our] heart' (Luke 6:45).

God wants to encourage and inform you through His Word. That's what the 'Food for thought' section is all about. It gives you the invaluable opportunity of hearing from God direct and of storing up what He says to you. **Please use a separate notebook** particularly for this section. Not only will it help you to crystallise your thoughts, but it will also be of tremendous reference value in the future.

As you study, refuse to let time pressurise you. Pray that God will speak to you personally and expect Him to do so. You may sometimes find that you're so enthralled by what He says to you that you're looking up many Scriptures which are not even suggested!

Finally, may God bless you as you work through this book. May He help you to understand His heart for the poor and to love them as He directs.

Remember the poor

Agabus stood up and through the Spirit predicted that a severe famine would spread over the entire Roman world. (This happened during the reign of Claudius.) The disciples, each according to his ability, decided to provide help for the brothers living in Judea. This they did, sending their gift to the elders by Barnabas and Saul (Acts 11:28–30).

The Council at Jerusalem was brought together to discuss a difficult issue: Should Gentile Christians 'be circumcised and required to obey the law of Moses' (Acts 15:5)? After some debate, those present decided, 'No,' but they did agree that the Gentiles should abstain from certain foods and sexual immorality. The conclusions were written down in a letter which was read by the Gentiles who were 'glad for its encouraging message' (Acts 15:31).

When Paul wrote to the Galatians, he touched on the controversy that was debated at Jerusalem (Gal. 2:1–10). But he also added something which was not recorded in Acts 15. Referring to the key members of the Jerusalem Church, he said, 'All they asked was that we should continue to remember the poor, the very thing I was eager to do' (Gal. 2:10).

From time to time God has challenged the Vineyard Church about the poor. On occasions, we've given thousands of dollars to disaster victims in places like Cambodia. And we've collected great quantities of food and clothing which we've sent to Mexico. Much of this work has been intermittent, but whenever there's been a need, we've tried to contribute to it.

▓ To ask

Why is it significant that the Council of Jerusalem asked Paul to remember the poor?

_____

_____

What significance does this have for Christians today?

_____

▓ To meditate on

The early church remembered the poor. 'There were no needy persons among them' (Acts 4:34).
'Tabitha ... was always doing good and helping the poor' (Acts 9:36).
'I came to Jerusalem to bring my people gifts for the poor and to present offerings' (Acts 24:17).
'Macedonia and Achaia were pleased to make a contribution for the poor among the saints in Jerusalem' (Rom. 15:26).

We've also helped the poor in our own country. Several years ago, we spent about eighteen months refurbishing homes. At one point, we were virtually rebuilding about a hundred properties — putting in new electrics, plumbing, floors, walls, ceilings and roofs. Sometimes we provided furnishings, fences and gates. We were doing all we could to make life easier for people with needs. We largely stopped the work when it became hard to find a house that needed repair!

Some time ago, the Governor of Southern California decided that many of the inmates in our state asylums should be getting their needs met through outside agencies. He therefore cut asylum funding in half which meant that scores of people with all kinds of mental illness were discharged and left to fend for themselves. We've ministered to hundreds of them, helped them to function within the economic system and led many to the Lord. But the fact remains that there are still thousands of people who have nowhere to go.

'All they asked was that we should continue to remember the poor,' said Paul. Increasingly it's the very thing I'm eager to do.

➢ Begin a research project into:

a) the needs among your community. (You can do this by gathering information from your local newspaper and through your own observation.)

b) how these needs are being met. (You could ring or write to any local charities and your local council to find out what programmes are running.)

➢ Compare your information. Is there a gap between the needs and the programmes? Begin to think about what you or your church could do about it.

▨ To ponder

In what ways can we remember the poor?

_____

_____

What is your church doing in each of these areas?

_____

_____

Bias to the poor sounds like a statement of political preference. My experience has been that some of the most central teachings of orthodox Christianity lead me to this position.
David Sheppard

Institution or organism?

'Love the Lord your
God with all your heart
and with all your soul
and with all your mind.'
This is the first and
greatest
commandment. And
the second is like it:
'Love your neighbour
as yourself'
(Matt. 22:37–39).

Many Christians confuse the church as an institution, with the church as an organism. In other words, they really haven't grasped how active the church's role should be in the community. Let me explain further.

On one occasion a man came up to me. He'd been trying to get hold of me for several days and had refused to talk to any of the other church leaders because he wanted to see 'The Pastor'. When he finally got hold of me he was incensed and his face was bright red as he poured out his tale of woe.

'I found this guy in the park,' he said. 'He was thin and dirty; he didn't have any decent clothes; he was sick and he was on drugs. I wanted to help him so I brought him here, but the church building was locked and there wasn't anyone around to meet his need. So I ended up taking him home, feeding and clothing him. He's been at my place for the last three days. I've been trying to get him to look for a job but he doesn't know how to work. He can't read or write and I don't know how to cope. Why isn't the church doing anything?'

I replied, 'It is. The church is picking up guys in the park, taking them home, feeding and

▓ To analyse

Be completely honest and analyse your reaction to someone you encounter who is homeless. (Think about a specific occasion in the past.)

Write down exactly what you thought about them.

_____

_____

▓ To meditate on

We must love others.
'Let no debt remain outstanding, except the continuing debt to love one another, for he who loves his fellow-man has fulfilled the law' (Rom. 13:8).
'Love your enemies, do good to those who hate you, bless those who curse you, pray for those who ill-treat you' (Luke 6:27,28).
'Let us consider how we may spur one another on towards love and good deeds' (Heb. 10:24).

clothing them and looking after their needs.' He looked at me as though I'd hit him in the face. Then he said, 'What do you mean?' And I replied, 'That's the church. That's what we're talking about.' His eyes sort of clouded with tears and he said, 'If that's the church, I don't think I like it!'

Everyone is happy to take care of the poor at a distance. But when the poor turn out to be half mad and want what you've got, then you withdraw. If it were easy to minister to those with needs, everyone would do it. But it's not, so very few are involved.

Materialism has gripped the church, yet the pursuit of things has brought not satisfaction but disappointment and a constant craving for something new to excite us. While we race off after personal satisfaction, thousands of desperate people roam the streets. Should we be looking to the government or the social services to meet their needs? No. The work should be spearheaded by the church.

God has been challenging me over all this. His Spirit is prompting me to cry out, 'Lord, stir up the church. Begin speaking to individuals. Let them understand your heart for the poor.'

▓ To discover

Look up the words *institution* and *organism* in a dictionary. What do each of these mean in the context of the church?

_____

_____

_____

▓ Food for thought

➤ Spend time seeking the Lord about your reactions to the poor.

➤ Ask Him to reveal any hidden prejudices you have.

➤ Ask Him to show you His heart for the poor.

➤ Ask Him to speak to you as you work through this study about what you should be doing to help the poor.

How does the Holy Spirit shape a living church? There is undoubtedly a many-faceted answer to that question. But I'm convinced He shapes primarily through people. The Antioch church became the greatest missionary church in the New Testament because God gave them the greatest missionaries. As a church we too are convinced that we should be doing whatever it is the Holy Spirit has laid on the hearts of the people whom He has sent to us.
Frank R. Tillapaugh

Are you really satisfied?

'I am the LORD your God, who brought you out of Egypt. You shall acknowledge no God but me, no Saviour except me. I cared for you in the desert, in the land of burning heat. When I fed them, they were satisfied; when they were satisfied, they became proud; then they forgot me' (Hos. 13:4–6).

At the time when I was asking God to stir the church about the needs of the poor, a young woman in our church came up to me and shared the following story. I hope it challenges and motivates you.

'A girlfriend and I were agreeing that we just couldn't go on living like "normal" Christians any more — just being satisfied with church on Sunday and living through the rest of the week. We were so stirred that we told God, "Whatever it takes, Lord, we want to do the work of the Kingdom. We want to go for it!"

'Suddenly God gave me a clear picture of a house in a run-down neighbourhood. I described the house to my friend and we drove to an area where we thought it might be. After about ten minutes going up and down various streets, we pulled over and there was the house, exactly as I'd described it.

'We got out of the car and asked a woman at the house what she did there. She told us that in about 1970 God had given her a dream and told her to set up a place from which she could help the poor. The day after she'd had the dream she collapsed from a heart attack and was hospitalised for a month. I believe that the

▓ To consider

Do you confine your Christian activity to meetings?

How are you living out your Christian life outside of church buildings?

_____

_____

_____

▓ To meditate on

Worldly pleasures don't satisfy.
'Whoever loves money never has money enough; whoever loves wealth is never satisfied with his income' (Eccl. 5:10).
'All man's efforts are for his mouth, yet his appetite is never satisfied' (Eccl. 6:7).
'Why spend money on what is not bread, and your labour on what does not satisfy?' (Isa. 55:2)

devil knew how effective her ministry was going to be and tried to stop her. He didn't succeed.

'When she'd recuperated she just threw herself into the work. Churches became interested and started donating money; stores began giving bread. "We get about two hundred people a day," she told us. "We feed and clothe them and give them whatever they need." My friend and I drove home, amazed at how God had shown us the house and equally amazed at the way that He was using this woman.

'About three weeks went by. Life was busy. I was going out; having fun, but somehow I didn't feel fulfilled. Then God reminded me about the house. I returned one Friday and spent a couple of hours feeding people there.

'As I was driving home God reminded me how many times that we as a church had said to Him, "Don't ever let us be satisfied with churchgoing and housegroups. We want to live our lives for you."

'He said that He had given many Christians a feeling of discontent because He wanted them to stop seeking fulfilment from normal earthly pleasures and to find new satisfaction and direction from Him.'

▓ Food for thought

➤ Read through Psalms 17:15; 63:1– 5; 90:14; 103:5; 107:9; Proverbs 13:4; Jeremiah 31:25.

➤ What does it mean to be satisfied?

➤ Where does our satisfaction come from?

➤ What is satisfying you at present — is it in line with these Scriptures?

▓ To respond

What is your response to the young woman's statement: 'Whatever it takes, Lord, we want to do the work of the Kingdom. We want to go for it!'?

Spend time talking this over with the Lord. Ask Him to show you areas in your life where you are holding back. Confess apathy. Tell the Lord you want to go for Him and ask Him to help you make the necessary changes to your life.

Jesus tells us that people who cry because their hearts are broken over the things that break the heart of God are the fulfilled people in this world.
Tom Sine

Catch God's heart

God presides in the great assembly; he gives judgment among the 'gods': 'How long will you defend the unjust and show partiality to the wicked? Defend the cause of the weak and fatherless; maintain the rights of the poor and oppressed. Rescue the weak and needy; deliver them from the hand of the wicked' (Ps. 82:1–4).

Psalm 82 is a lament and an exhortation. It begins by mourning the condition of the 'great assembly' where the 'gods' judge. The 'gods' could be interpreted to refer to leaders who are not properly attuned to the Lord's value system. They're showing partiality to the wicked and unjustly treating everyone else.

The second part of the Psalm is an appeal to them to acknowledge what's happening and to do something about it. This appeal is eventually directed to God.

Many of the heartbreaks in the church come because leaders are running organisational structures rather than living organisms. They're trying to maintain the machinery rather than respond to the present word from God. If you introduce some zealous believer into this atmosphere, he will not be commended for his inner devotion, but judged for his outer attitude and appropriately, and unjustly, muzzled.

How do we defend the cause of the weak and fatherless? You don't work through a structure but through a living body. The young man in Study 2 didn't realise this. He thought of the church as a organisation, not as a company of people who laid down their lives for others.

▓ To determine

We all make judgements in life.

What kind of judgements are right?

_____

What kind of judgements are wrong?

_____

What are both these kinds of judgements based on?

_____

▓ To meditate on

We must watch how we judge.
'In the same way as you judge others, you will be judged' (Matt. 7:2).
'Stop judging by mere appearances, and make a right judgment' (John 7:24).
'Why do you judge your brother? Or why do you look down on your brother?' (Rom. 14:10)
'Judgment without mercy will be shown to anyone who has not been merciful' (James 2:13).

When I was a new Christian I went to a downtown mission in Los Angeles and was very offended that the believers there preached to the people before they fed them. I was told that if the order were reversed, many would fall asleep. I didn't agree and was angry about it. But I soon realised that I was wrong.

Those believers had been faithfully serving over many years. They understood the different individuals. Who was I to correct them? I had the programme; but they had the relationship. I wanted to minister from the head; they were ministering from the heart. I'd completely failed to see what was going on.

We will never step out of our middle-class strategy and do anything for the poor until we've caught God's heart for them.

I once watched a documentary about people who were ministering to those on the streets. Mentally I considered my busy schedule and bitterly regretted that I'd allowed so many things to crowd out God's higher priorities. I didn't have time for the poor. As I sat there I wept and prayed, 'Oh God, I feel so bad about this. I want my calendar to change. Please help me to organise my life around Your heart.'

▓ Food for thought

➤ In two columns in your notebook draw up lists of the characteristics of:

a) someone who is poor.

b) someone who is affluent.

➤ What does the Lord look at when He judges a man?

➤ What difference in heart is there (if any) between your two lists?

➤ Ask the Lord to show you if you are guilty of making wrong judgements of poor people. Ask Him to reveal His heart towards the poor to you.

▓ To review

Review all your commitments: church, family, work, etc.

Which of these are organised around God's heart and priorities?

Write down what changes you need to make and how you will do this.

_____

_____

If we are going to have the same dramatic impact that Jesus had on his community, then we must follow his example of involvement. We cannot do it vicariously through others. We must get involved ourselves.
Dave Andrews

Will your work stand?

'They know nothing, they understand nothing. They walk about in darkness; all the foundations of the earth are shaken. I said, "You are 'gods': you are all sons of the Most High." But you will die like mere men; you will fall like every other ruler.' Rise up, O God, judge the earth, for all the nations are your inheritance (Ps. 82:5–8).

Asaph, the writer of Psalm 82, goes on to consider the sad situation of the ordinary people who probably think that they're enlightened but who are actually walking in darkness, blindly repeating the same mistakes. And he looks at their oppressors — those 'gods' in leadership whose resources will dry up and whose institutions will fall.

Any church that is not built on God's foundation is standing on sand. One day it will collapse. You only have to look around to see the truth of this. Church buildings have been converted into community centres, jumble sale venues and bingo halls. Hundreds remain empty because no one can think of what to do with them. I'm sure that each pastor once said, 'We're going to establish a great work in this place. Now bring your offerings.' So everyone saved and gave and tried to develop the work. Then they moved away or grew old and died. And they left behind a derelict monument.

We can share the righteous anger that burns in Asaph's soul as he appeals to God to judge the nations. The institutions of men must be weighed on His scale. These include economic systems and governments, companies and

▓ To analyse

Write down any reasons you have had for not ministering to the poor.

_____

_____

_____

Do any of these stand up to the Word of God?

▓ To meditate on

God weighs and judges.
'The LORD is a God who knows, and by him deeds are weighed' (1 Sam. 2:3).
'Let God weigh me in honest scales and he will know that I am blameless' (Job. 31:6).
'All a man's ways seem innocent to him, but motives are weighed by the LORD' (Prov. 16:2).
'You have been weighed ... and found wanting' (Dan. 5:27).

churches. Jesus will judge them all. In the light of this, I don't plan to get involved in political campaigns and other side-issues. I want to hear the Word of the Lord and to act on it.

God's heart is broken over the poor, the helpless, the oppressed, the homeless and the mentally ill. If your timetable makes no room for them, you must reconsider it. Countless generations have heard that God cares for the needy and wants His people to reach out to them. Few people have obeyed.

Today God looks for individuals who listen to His Word and respond to it. 'Remember the poor,' He says. 'Preach to them; lead them to Jesus; cast out their demons; minister to their physical and emotional needs; help them to find employment and show them the way through the bureaucratic maze in your nation.'

One day you will appear before God and your works will be weighed. Jesus won't give you a theological exam and question you about your views on the pre-tribulation rapture. He'll ask you what you did for the hungry, the thirsty, the strangers, the sick and the imprisoned. Wouldn't you love to hear His 'Well done — whatever you did for them, you did for Me'?

▓ Food for thought

➤ Read Matthew 25:31–46.

➤ What is the context of this parable?

➤ What motivation to minister to the poor does it reveal?

➤ Think of practical ways in which you personally can feed the hungry, give water to the thirsty, invite the stranger, clothe the needy and visit the sick or imprisoned.

▓ To compare

Jesus said that He was anointed 'to preach good news to the poor' (Luke 4:18).

What does that 'good news' consist of?

_____

_____

How does this compare with your understanding of the gospel?

Renewed faith in the great hope that God's Kingdom will be established and recognised everywhere, brings with it the sense of urgency in reaching as many of the lost as possible with the truth, so that they may have opportunity to repent of their sins and be born again into the Kingdom of God.
Colin Urquhart

Protector of the poor

'Because of the oppression of the weak and the groaning of the needy, I will now arise,' says the LORD. 'I will protect them from those who malign them' (Ps. 12:5).

He will defend the afflicted among the people and save the children of the needy; he will crush the oppressor (Ps. 72:4).

Since the Old Testament contains more instruction about reaching out to the poor than the New, we might conclude that God was more concerned about the underprivileged then, than He is today. This is not the case.

The Israelites were under law and were given rules. We're under grace and have the direct guidance of the Holy Spirit. He underlines the principles in the Old Testament, points to Jesus' example and warns us through several New Testament Scriptures not to harden our hearts against the poor. So God's attitude has never changed. What He set down for the Israelites He also lays before the church.

In the Old Testament there are several words concerning the poor that share the same Hebrew root. In English they're translated: weak, helpless, impoverished, oppressed and needy. In God's eyes, these various aspects of poverty illustrate what it feels like to be poor.

I've found about thirty verses in which the Lord tells us that He will be the protector of the poor. He has set Himself up as judge over the affairs of men — particularly to rescue them from oppression. He watches when employers line their own pockets and fail to pay their

▓ **To analyse**

In our society who would you consider to be:

the weak _____

the helpless _____

the impoverished _____

the oppressed _____

the needy? _____

▓ **To meditate on**

Nothing is hidden from God's sight. 'From heaven the LORD looks down and sees all mankind ... he watches all who live on earth (and) considers everything they do' (Ps. 33:13–15).
'The LORD watches over the alien and sustains the fatherless and the widow, but he frustrates the ways of the wicked' (Ps. 146:9).
'The eyes of the LORD are everywhere, keeping watch on the wicked and the good' (Prov. 15:3).

workers a just wage. He notices the landlords who demand exorbitant rents from their tenants. He sees those who sell substandard goods which look like bargains but which will fall apart in no time.

The poor can appeal to men. They can cry out to their neighbours and friends and to the political mechanisms that are available. But they can also go over the heads of these people and present their case directly to God. He will listen to them and defend their cause.

Later I want to consider more closely the subject of justice. But for the moment, I'm keen that we see our responsibility to relieve the poor and to enhance their circumstances. Not only must we feed and clothe them, we must also help them to get good jobs so that they can participate in our economy.

The principle is always the same: you give someone a fish, teach him to fish for himself and finally give him a licence so that he can fish whenever he likes. Many churches have got as far as phase one. But we need to progress beyond that. The poor don't just cry out for immediate relief. They want to be integrated into society — just like everyone else.

▓ Food for thought

➤ Christians throughout history have worked to improve the conditions and circumstances of the poor.

➤ Try to get hold of a biography of William Wilberforce, General Booth, Jackie Pullinger-To, or other Christians working with the poor.

➤ Make notes on:

- what motivated them,
- what their characters were like,
- what kept them going,
- how they formed their strategies.

▓ To study

Read Deuteronomy 15:1–11.

What commands does God give?

_____

_____

_____

Are you tight-fisted or open-handed towards the poor?

Poverty is more than just having no money; it is not having the freedom to make choices about one's destiny.
Floyd McClung Jr.

Provider for the poor

At the end of every three years, bring all the tithes of that year's produce ... so that the Levites ... and the aliens, the fatherless and the widows ... may come and eat and be satisfied
(Deut. 14:28,29).

'Do not reap to the very edges of your field or gather the gleanings of your harvest. Do not go over your vineyard a second time or pick up the grapes that have fallen. Leave them for the poor and the alien.'
(Lev. 19:9,10).

'During the seventh year let the land lie unploughed and unused. Then the poor ... may get food from it'
(Exod. 23:11).

I n the Old Testament, God made special provision for the poor. For a start, there was the third-year tithe. Every three years the Israelites were commanded to store this in their towns for the Levites and the poor. It was the welfare system of the day — the means by which the people were blessed.

Our tax system is a kind of parallel with this. When we pay our taxes we're complying with Scripture because a certain amount of the money that we hand over is allocated to the welfare of the country. So we're effectively giving to God for His purposes.

Like you, perhaps, I'm not sure that the revenue is always used wisely. I don't want to heap curses on the Treasury, but neither do I want to be held responsible for any unjust actions. So I pray, 'Lord, I want to be an obedient citizen so I'll gladly pay my taxes. But if the government doesn't handle the money right, you deal with them. I leave the matter in your hands.'

God provided for the poor in other ways too. He prevented them from being overwhelmed by debt in that He told the lenders to write off all outstanding debts in the seventh year. And He

▓ To determine

Determine ways in which you can leave the 'the gleanings of your harvest' (Lev. 19:9 see above) for the poor, e.g. give away the interest earned on savings.

Put your ideas into practice as soon as possible.

▓ To meditate on

God provides for the poor.
'The poor will eat and be satisfied' (Ps. 22:26).
'From your bounty, O God, you provided for the poor' (Ps. 68:10).
'He has scattered abroad his gifts to the poor' (Ps. 112:9).
'He raises the poor from the dust and lifts the needy from the ash heap' (Ps. 113:7).
'(Zion's) poor will I satisfy with food' (Ps. 132:15).

ensured that the poor always had a harvest by commanding the farmers not to reap to the edges of their fields.

Every seven years the farmers were required not to sow and reap. Since there would be seed in the soil from the sixth year, there would be a harvest, but it wouldn't be as plentiful as before. Whatever grew — crops, grapes or olives — would be given exclusively to the poor.

Sometimes it may be appropriate to give all the yield of something to the poor. We've discovered that at the Vineyard. When God told us to move, we knew that we'd need a staggering $15 million. 'Take up an offering,' God said. And I thought, 'Fine.' Then He added, 'And give it all to the poor.'

God has tested me like this on many occasions. Even though I know what He wants me to do, I still get nervous because as leader of the church, I'm the one who has the final responsibility. So at first I couldn't believe what I was hearing. My logic told me to pay off as much of the debt as soon as we could. But that wasn't God's economy. His heart was with the poor and after a while, it began to sound right to give the firstfruits to them.

✱ Food for thought

➤ Read Leviticus 25.

➤ What effect would the year of Jubilee have on:

- the acquisition of wealth
- the poor
- class structure?

➤ What immediate effect would there be on our nation if this year was proclaimed a year of Jubilee?

✱ To discover

What is your attitude towards paying tax?

Look up Matthew 17:24–27 and Romans 13:6,7.

What do these verses teach about paying tax?

_____

_____

_____

For it is not primarily the wealthy and the famous with whom he (God) delights to fraternize. What is characteristic of him is to champion the poor, to rescue them from their misery, and to transform paupers into princes.
John Stott

Self-induced poverty

Diligent hands will rule,
but laziness ends in
slave labour
(Prov. 12:24).

He who ignores
discipline comes to
poverty and shame
(Prov. 13:18).

The plans of the diligent
lead to profit as surely
as haste leads to
poverty (Prov. 21:5).

Drunkards and gluttons
become poor, and
drowsiness clothes
them in rags
(Prov. 23:21).

Poor people aren't necessarily the victims of circumstances. Sometimes they have themselves to blame. Proverbs warns us about behaviour that will ultimately result in poverty.

Laziness. It isn't wise to be lazy, because sluggishness has its own recompense — and that's powerful. If people aren't diligent, they'll be doubly impoverished. First, they'll find themselves financially insolvent and second, they will become slaves to those who do work hard. These masters will extract from them the last drop of energy that they have.

Foolishness. Undisciplined behaviour also leads to poverty. Foolish people don't take the advice of others, persist in unwise courses of action and rationalise to cover their tracks. The poor are steeped in rationalisation. Everyone else is to blame but them. 'I wouldn't be here if he hadn't ...' they say.

Naturally, we must be warm and kind when we're dealing with them, but we mustn't be blind to their excuses. We can give them 'phase one' help — food, clothing and maybe a place to stay — but if we want to move them into phases two and three, we will have to say, 'Right, we can give you immediate assistance,

▓ To pray

Pray for any Christian organisations you know which are helping to rehabilitate people with addictions.

Ask the Lord if you should become involved in giving, prayer, voluntary work, etc. to support them.

▓ To meditate on

We must choose: diligence or laziness. 'Whatever the God of heaven has prescribed, let it be done with diligence for the temple of the God of heaven' (Ezra 7:23).
'The sluggard craves and gets nothing, but the desires of the diligent are fully satisfied' (Prov. 13:4).
'We want each of you to show ... diligence to the very end, in order to make your hope sure. We do not want you to become lazy' (Heb. 6:11,12).

but if you take responsibility for ... then we can do this ...' If they're unwilling to respond to discipline, then we can do no more for them.

Undisciplined decision-making. Impoverished people repeatedly make bad decisions. It's easy to chastise them, 'That was a really stupid thing to do. Why did you do it?' But this sort of unchristlike attitude won't help them or us. It would be better if we got alongside them and said, 'Now, you've been making these kinds of decisions for a number of years and that's why you're still in your situation. I can't make up your mind for you, but maybe I could teach you how to think things through for yourself and find your own way out of poverty.'

Drunkenness. People are often poor as a result of excesses in their lives. They're hooked on alcohol, drugs, cigarettes and compulsions like gambling — things which have dire financial consequences.

Although the Bible doesn't say, 'You mustn't drink alcohol', we must remember that we're surrounded by alcoholism and are responsible to others in this matter. Let's not make them stumble by what we do. Each of us must work this through in good conscience before God.

▓ Food for thought

➤ Meditate on Jesus' commandment 'Love your neighbour as yourself.'

➤ Write down your thoughts on what this means to you.

_____

_____

_____

_____

➤ Read Luke 10:25–37 to stimulate ideas.

▓ To consider

Make a list of practical ways in which *you* can give phase one help. Try to think beyond giving money, e.g. carry sandwiches or food vouchers with you on shopping trips where you will encounter people begging.

_____

_____

_____

_____

Street people can often be lazy, angry, ungrateful, uncouth, undisciplined, unprincipled, and arrogant. They are often not an easy bunch to share life with. Yet I can't help but believe that if Jesus were on earth today one of the first groups He would target would be street people.
Frank R. Tillapaugh

Good news for the poor

'God so loved the world that he gave his one and only Son, that whoever believes in him shall not perish but have eternal life' (John 3:16).

You know the grace of our Lord Jesus Christ, that though he was rich, yet for your sakes he became poor, so that you through his poverty might become rich (2 Cor. 8:9).

'The Spirit of the Lord is on me, because he has anointed me to preach good news to the poor' (Luke 4:18).

Almost every time the word 'poor' is used in the Bible, it means the 'oppressed poor'. Sometimes that oppression is self-induced; on other occasions it manifests itself through the harsh treatment of others.

So far we've focused primarily on God's commands to the Israelites to reach out to the needy. But as I've already said, God is just as concerned that the New Testament church should continue to 'remember the poor'.

God remembers the poor. He knew about our wretchedness and inability to help ourselves and was moved to intervene. So He sent His Son — the One through whom He created the universe — to free us from our sin. Jesus didn't suddenly arrive in the world as a mighty king and take up residence in a fabulous palace. He came as a tiny baby and was born into a poor household. His identification with the poor demonstrates His great love for us and breaks the heart of every believer in time and eternity.

Jesus announced the nature of His mission in Luke 4 — to preach good news to the poor. This 'good news' concerned the breakthrough of the Kingdom of God. If people repented and believed the gospel, He would change them into

▓ To ask

Read Isaiah 61:1–3 and Luke 4:18,19. What are the characteristics of the Kingdom?

_____

_____

Are you preaching every aspect of the kingdom? Pray for a full manifestation of the Kingdom in your area.

▓ To meditate on

Jesus is the last Adam.
'Death reigned from the time of Adam to the time of Moses, even over those who did not sin by breaking a command, as did Adam, who was a pattern of the one to come' (Rom. 5:14). 'As in Adam all die, so in Christ all will be made alive ... just as we have borne the likeness of the earthly man, so shall we bear the likeness of the man from heaven' (1 Cor. 15:22,49).

new creations (2 Cor. 5:17) and rule in their hearts. What Adam had lost, Jesus would win back. Poverty would be turned into riches through faith in Christ.

When John's disciples asked Jesus, 'Are you the one who was to come?' the Lord didn't only point them to His miracles as proof of His Messiahship, but also to the fact that 'the good news is preached to the poor' (Luke 7:22). The proclamation of the gospel to the poor was one of the signs of the presence of the Kingdom.

Not only did Jesus bring the Word of God, He also performed the works of God. He taught the message of the Kingdom in what He said and did. If we say to someone, 'Go, I wish you well; keep warm and well fed' (James 2:16) but do nothing at all about his physical needs, we're preaching an incomplete gospel. Jesus wants to relieve suffering, heal and deliver as well as save. We must bring the mercy of God to bear on all the circumstances of life.

'Blessed are you who are poor,' said Jesus, 'for yours is the kingdom of God' (Luke 6:20). It's a glorious promise. If the poor receive the message of salvation, they can enjoy the Kingdom both now and in eternity.

▓ Food for thought

➤ Imagine yourself confronted by a homeless person on the street and think about how you would go about sharing the gospel with him/her.

➤ Consider the language you would use.

➤ What practical considerations could there be?

➤ Do you think that if you fed them first they would be more or less likely to listen to the gospel?

➤ Is it necessary to preach the gospel in words?

▓ To consider

The gospel to the poor is integral to the presence of the Kingdom.

One of the results of putting our faith in God should be loving our neighbour (or good works).

Why do you think so many Christians/churches do not make a ministry to the poor a priority?

Jesus both 'went about ... teaching ... and preaching' (Matt. 4:23, 9:35 RSV) and 'went about doing good and healing' (Acts 10:38 RSV). In consequence, 'evangelism and social concern have been intimately related to one another throughout the history of the Church'.
John Stott

Your Kingdom come

'Anyone who has faith in me will do what I have been doing. He will do even greater things than these' (John 14:12).

Continue to work out your salvation with fear and trembling, for it is God who works in you to will and to act according to his good purpose (Phil. 2:12).

Sometimes there is a tendency to emphasise the importance of salvation by faith to such an extent that good works seem to be almost irrelevant for the believer.

The Scriptures, however, often emphasise the importance of faith and works. The Christian life is not about holding onto our salvation; it's about working out our salvation. It's not primarily about having a good time while we wait for our call to heaven; it's about getting on with establishing the Kingdom of God on earth.

Now the Kingdom and the church are not one and the same thing. The church is the community of the Kingdom. The Kingdom is the reign of God — which is far greater. In the Lord's Prayer, Jesus exhorts us to pray to the Father, 'your kingdom come, your will be done on earth as it is in heaven' (Matt. 6:10).

The Kingdom and the will of God operate together. You can tell when the Kingdom is present in a situation when you see harmony in it — people are right with God and with one another. When you don't see harmony, it's a clear sign that God's rule has been thwarted and something must be done about it.

▓ To memorise

Memorise Deuteronomy 15:10.

'Give generously to him (your needy brother) and do so without a grudging heart; then because of this the LORD your God will bless you in all your work and in everything you put your hand to.'

▓ To meditate on

Faith and works operate together.
'I worked harder than all of them — yet not I, but the grace of God that was with me' (1 Cor. 15:10).
'We continually remember before our God and Father your work produced by faith' (1 Thess. 1:3).
'God's work ... is by faith' (1 Tim. 1:4).
'(Abraham's) faith and his actions were working together, and his faith was made complete by what he did' (James 2:22).

Jesus wants us to be involved in bringing in His Kingdom. This means that whenever we see things that don't harmonise with the will of God, we combine faith and works — we pray for His Kingdom to come and do something to alleviate the problem.

In the parable of the sheep and the goats, Jesus deals with issues that don't reflect the Kingdom — poverty, alienation, sickness and imprisonment. As judge, He examines the responses of those who were close enough to these things to do something about them. Did they seek to establish His Kingdom or not?

The group that He commends are the 'sheep'. 'Come, you who are blessed by my Father,' He says, 'take your inheritance ... For I was hungry and you gave me something to eat ...' (Matt. 25:34,35).

The word 'For' here connects the blessing of God with the works of the people. Those who enjoy the favour of God are the individuals who are reaching out to others in practical ways. They realise that they're channels of God's love to the world. They want His will to be done on earth as it is in heaven and they're prepared to do something about it.

➢ Read Hebrews 11:6; James 2:14–16 and 1 John 3:16–18. What is the value of faith without works?

➢ What is the value of works without faith? What is the value of words without action?

➢ In what way do these passages challenge you?

➢ Spend time with the Lord talking over these issues.

❋ To do

Write down three examples of how we can combine faith and works.

_____

_____

_____

The church today can derive its sense of intention, direction, and mission directly from what Scripture tells us about the future intentions of God. Remarkably, God invites us, his children, to join with him in working for his intentions now. He calls us to work for righteousness, justice, peace, reconciliation, wholeness, and love. That is the mission of the church today ... to seek first his kingdom.
Tom Sine

☐ STUDY 11

Secret history before God

At Caesarea there was a man named Cornelius ... He and all his family were devout and God-fearing; he gave generously to those in need and prayed to God regularly. One day ... he had a vision. He distinctly saw an angel of God, who came to him and said ... 'Your prayers and gifts to the poor have come up as a memorial offering before God ...'
(See Acts 10:1–4).

Cornelius was devout. He hadn't received a personal revelation of Christ but he was faithfully doing many of the kind of things that Christians have yet to take on board. We're told that he prayed and gave generously to the poor. Clearly he was someone who wanted to live with a good conscience before the Lord.

God wasn't unaware of this man's devotion. On the contrary, his prayers and compassion for the needy had deeply impressed the Lord. So He sent an angel to commend Cornelius for his actions and to help him to discover the way of salvation. Later, both Cornelius and his household were saved and filled with the Spirit.

As an unbeliever, Cornelius didn't go around thinking, 'If I get up and pray for two hours a day, the Lord is bound to notice and send His angel to bless me.' And he didn't think, 'There's a lady down the street who's hurting, so I'll do this and that for her — and maybe God will reward me with a new Cadillac.' He didn't pray or give to manipulate God or impress others. He reached out because he wanted to know the Lord and to help those who were in need.

Jesus exhorted His disciples to have a secret history before God. 'When you give, pray and

▨ To review

How secret is your secret history before God?!

Spend time reviewing every area of your own devotional life and giving.

Set yourself realistic goals to make any changes you feel are necessary.

▨ To meditate on

God will always reward.
'What is due to me is in the LORD's hand, and my reward is with my God' (Isa. 49:4).
'I the LORD search the heart and examine the mind, to reward a man according to his conduct, according to what his deeds deserve' (Jer. 17:10).
'Watch out that you do not lose what you have worked for, but that you may be rewarded fully' (2 John 8).

'ast, don't let anyone know about it,' He said. 'If you do your acts of righteousness before men, the world may praise you, but there will be no reward from heaven.'

Today many people seek earthly acclaim. The more famous of them might decide to phone up the newspapers, get their photos taken and give fabulous sums of money to some charity or other. The next morning their names are blazed across the press for all to see. Those who aren't quite so wealthy still seek recognition from others but they do it in a more subtle way — maybe 'letting something slip' concerning the good that they've done.

Christians aren't exempt from the desire to be noticed by others. Secretly we often want people to know how prayerful and generous we are and find it hard simply to maintain a secret life of devotion before God.

When we announce our acts of righteousness to others, we demonstrate that we want our reward from God in the here and now. If that's what you're after, that's what God will give you. But don't you think you'd be more fulfilled if you set your sights on an eternal reward and lived for that instead?

▓ Food for thought

➢ Read Matthew 6:1–18.

➢ In what ways do some Christians today perform their 'acts of righteousness' before men:

- when they give to the needy,
- when they pray,
- when they fast?

➢ What is their motivation? Are you ever guilty of such things?

➢ How can you make sure that your acts of righteousness are secret?

▓ To do

In a notebook write down the word 'compassion' in the centre of a page.

Write other words around the word 'compassion' which have a similar meaning.

When you have built up a picture, write out your own definition of 'compassion'.

Service means obedience. By obedience to the ways of God we come to know the heart of God. By entering the heart of God we are enabled to be of help to people. Wholeness reigns in us, which means effective service for others.
Richard J. Foster

Open your hand

Do not be hard-hearted or tight-fisted towards your poor brother. Rather be open-handed and freely lend him whatever he needs. Be careful not to harbour this wicked thought: 'The seventh year, the year for cancelling debts, is near,' so that you do not show ill will towards your needy brother and give him nothing. He may then appeal to the LORD against you, and you will be found guilty of sin. Give generously to him and do so without a grudging heart; then your God will bless you in all your work and in everything you put your hand to
(Deut. 15:7–10).

Deuteronomy 15:7–11 shows us that from the very outset, God wanted His people to be generous to the poor.

When I'd been a Christian for about a year I remember wanting to do something for the needy and praying for direction about it. At the time I could have been thought of as poor. I was married and had four children aged six or under. I'd also been out of work for several months and my new job gave me only $87 a week clear — and I was tithing that.

As I prayed, God showed me a picture of a hand which was closed at first but which opened up. He then seemed to say, 'The world tells you to have a tight-fisted hand — particularly if you're in need yourself. It says you've got to cling to everything you've got. It advocates a logical and sensible economy. But that economy is not Mine. I want you to see that everything is in My control and to live with an open hand. If you do that, I will give you ample resources both for yourself and for others.'

The Israelites knew that in the seventh year the law required them to cancel all debts. So if you were an Israelite and if someone asked you

▓ To review

Look up Luke 12:22–32.

Are you trusting the Lord for this kind of provision?

Ask the Lord for more faith in the area of your finances.

Begin to step out in small ways and see the Lord meet your needs.

▓ To meditate on

Generosity reaps a reward.
'Give, and it will be given to you. A good measure, pressed down, shaken together and running over, will be poured into your lap. For with the measure you use, it will be measured to you' (Luke 6:38).
'Out of the most severe trial ... their extreme poverty welled up in rich generosity ... For they gave as much as they were able, and even beyond their ability' (2 Cor. 8:2,3).

for a loan in the sixth year, you might think, I'm only going to get a tiny portion of this back, so I'm not going to lend him anything. Let him approach me again in twelve months' time.' This attitude may seem justified in the world's economy, but it is sinful in God's eyes. If the needy person cries out against you, the Lord will hear him and hold you accountable.

God's way is to encourage you to give and then to load you with blessing. I've seen it happen both in my own life and in the lives of others. People have opened up their hearts and homes. They've given as generously as they possibly can, and God has caught up with them. He has met their needs and lavished His riches on them. They've been overtaken by abundance.

Deuteronomy 15 tells us that if we are generous to the poor, God will bless us. Our motivation to give shouldn't stem from the desire to receive. We should simply want to obey God's command regardless of whether He rewards us or not. But the fact remains that if we open our hands to the needy, He will bless us in all our work and in everything we put our hand to.

➢ Start some research into how you can give to the poor.

➢ Find out about the needs of:

- local and national charities,
- the poor fund (or similar) in your own church,
- covenanting to a particular project, etc. (if you are a tax payer).

➢ Pray that the Lord will show you how much to give and who to give it to.

▓ To analyse

Tight-fisted   Open-handed

|_____|

Mark on the line above the point where you feel you stand in your giving to the poor.
What needs to happen for you to be able to put your mark on 'open-handed'?

_____

What do you propose to do about this?

_____

Deep down inside most Christians I know is a deep-seated desire to release instead of keep ... to give instead of grab ... Become a giver ... and watch God open the hearts of others to Himself. We are never more Godlike than when we give.
Charles Swindoll

God or mammon?

Keep your lives free from the love of money and be content with what you have, because God has said, 'Never will I leave you; never will I forsake you.' So we say with confidence, 'The Lord is my helper; I will not be afraid. What can man do to me?' (Heb. 13:5,6).

Question: why do we hold back from giving to God's work? Answer: we love mammon. Society tells us that when the economy is in a state, we must respond by cutting back — or we won't have enough. 'You can't possibly give more,' people say. 'Don't take the risk — you'll regret it.' So we hold on to what we've got.

Some very famous people once did that. They were terrified that they wouldn't have enough, so they stored up their wealth. But far from giving them happiness, it made them miserable. Their money controlled them. They died imprisoned by their anxieties — rich in the eyes of the world, but poor in the opinion of God.

Many of us aren't involved in flagrant sins like immorality, drunkenness, stealing and lying, but we're bowing down to another, more subtle enemy. We're worshipping at the temple of mammon. 'I must have prestige and identity,' we say, so we focus our attention on our clothes, our possessions, our cars and our houses. Mammon tells us, 'You must ensure that you have enough to get all you want' and we all too readily agree.

Our savings and possessions become our idols. The more of them we have, the greater

▓ To assess

Make an honest assessment of where your security lies.

Is it fully in the Lord or is it in your possessions, income, etc.?

Ask the Lord to reveal to you any hold that materialism has over you. Take steps to deal with it.

▓ To meditate on

Beware of greed.
'You clean the outside of the cup and dish, but inside they are full of greed and self-indulgence' (Matt. 23:25).
'Watch out! Be on your guard against all kinds of greed; a man's life does not consist in the abundance of his possessions' (Luke 12:15).
'No immoral, impure or greedy person — such a man is an idolater — has any inheritance in the kingdom of Christ and of God' (Eph. 5:5).

our sense of security becomes, and the more we're entrenched in materialism. Then when God challenges us about being generous, we panic, give away a small sum and cling like crazy to the rest.

God wants to break us out of this. How can He reach the poor when we're so greedy for gain? How can He be our security when we're so caught up with the god of this world? How can He prove that He'll supply all our needs if we're not willing to launch out and give?

We can't serve God and mammon. We can't listen to messages from the world which advertise extreme caution when the Word of God advocates extreme liberality. The two are mutually exclusive. Either we follow one or the other. There's no middle way.

It's time we realised that we're citizens of heaven and sojourners on the earth. One day, the world will burn up and all our savings and possessions will go with it. In the light of this, does it really matter what clothes we're wearing; what luxuries we're enjoying; what car we're driving; or where we're living? Isn't it more important that we pour our lives into things that are going to last for ever?

▓ Food for thought

➤ Read Haggai 1.

➤ What were the people doing?

➤ What did the Lord want them to do?

➤ What were the results of their living for the now instead of for eternity?

▓ To answer

Read 2 Corinthians 4:17—5:1.

In practical terms, how can we live for eternity?

Give at least three examples in everyday life.

_____

_____

_____

Mammon is the Aramaic term for "wealth, money, property, or profit." The fascinating truth here is that Jesus elevates money to divine status. He places it right up on par with God. It more than anything else can act like a god.
Donald B. Kraybill

How to make money

See that you ... excel in this grace of giving (2 Cor. 8:7).

I have never seen the righteous forsaken or their children begging bread. They are always generous and lend freely; their children will be blessed (Ps. 37:25,26).

Christians must learn how to be generous. Church leaders often stress tithing — and I guess that's a good place to start. But I feel that the New Testament teaching goes far beyond the traditional tithe — which can actually become a very mechanical operation.

Some of us look at our giving in a legalistic, self-satisfied way. 'I give my tithe' we declare smugly, and avoid any emotional involvement in the need. Others of us are so motivated by the grace of God that we can't stop ourselves pouring our resources into the Kingdom. We see a need and immediately we're asking ourselves, 'What can I do to meet it?'

Back in 1964 I was earning $90,000 a year. Then I became a Christian and it wasn't long before my salary had dropped to $700 a month. For about three years Carol and I really had to battle through our finances. But during that time, God began teaching us about giving. 'The way to make money in the Kingdom is to give it away,' He told us. 'Start giving and I'll meet all your needs.'

It was really hard. Sometimes we were praying about whether we could afford to donate an extra 50 cents — that's how tight it

▦ To do

Give something (money, food parcel, gift, clothing, etc.) to someone you know who is in need.

▦ To meditate on

Our attitude as we give is important. 'Freely you have received, freely give' (Matt. 10:8).
'Finish the arrangements for the generous gift you had promised. Then it will be ready as a generous gift, not as one grudgingly given ... Each man should give what he has decided in his heart to give, not reluctantly or under compulsion, for God loves a cheerful giver' (2 Cor. 9:5,7).

was. But as we gave, God started to bless. In a short time, we'd paid off all our debts and in the fifth or sixth year we had more than we needed. So we multiplied our giving and God multiplied His return.

The principle is just the same for churches as it is for individuals. Our ministry to the poor began really small. We chose a spot from which we could distribute food and clothing and we changed its location as the work grew. Now we've got a warehouse that measures 17,000 square feet. And big donors are coming and asking if we'll let them support us. As we've repeatedly increased our giving, God has opened the windows of heaven and rained down His blessings on us.

As we draw near to God, we will naturally become more generous. His heart of love for people will ignite ours and we'll stop living selfishly and begin looking for ways in which we can bless others.

Let's pull away from the grip of materialism and cultivate a spirit of generosity. Only as we do this will we realise the truth of Jesus' words, 'It is more blessed to give than to receive' (Acts 20:35).

▓ To decide

Write down what you personally need to do in order to cultivate a generous spirit, e.g. cut back on non-essentials, walk instead of catch the bus, give away savings, etc.

_____

_____

_____

▓ Food for thought

➤ Read John 12:1–8.

➤ Divide a page in your notebook into two columns and compare Mary and Judas.

➤ Which of them do you most resemble?

The matter of stewardship of money is fundamental to Christian growth.
R. T. Kendall

Something far better

By faith Moses, when he had grown up, refused to be known as the son of Pharaoh's daughter. He chose to be ill-treated along with the people of God rather than to enjoy the pleasures of sin for a short time. He regarded disgrace for the sake of Christ as of greater value than the treasures of Egypt, because he was looking ahead to his reward (Heb. 11:24–26).

J esus frequently challenged the world's economy. On one occasion He told His host to invite to his home not his friends but the poor. Jesus wasn't prohibiting meals with friends — He Himself was happy to eat with anyone. It's just that this 'prominent Pharisee' (Luke 14:1) evidently needed to associate with the sort of guests whom he would normally never invite — those who couldn't repay him. There are several New Testament illustrations of people who either clung to the natural economy or embraced the economy of God.

The rich young ruler stuck with a 'safe' economy. Jesus told him that if he sold his possessions and gave the money to the poor he would have treasure in heaven — but he couldn't relate to that. He was frightened at the prospect of liquidating his assets and living for the future. His focus was on the letter of the law, not the spirit of it. So he walked away sad.

Zacchaeus on the other hand completely understood the economy of God. He too was wealthy, but as a tax collector, he was also unpopular.

Jesus called Zacchaeus by name and identified Himself with what the people called a

▓ To seek

Spend 20 minutes seeking the Lord for His compassion and for a heart of mercy towards the poor.

Ask Him to soften your heart, repent of any bad attitudes to the poor and express your desire to be more like Jesus.

▓ To meditate on

A merciful God calls us to be merciful. 'Blessed are the merciful, for they will be shown mercy' (Matt. 5:7).
'Shouldn't you have had mercy on you fellow-servant just as I had on you?' (Matt. 18:33)
'Be merciful, just as your Father is merciful' (Luke 6:36).
'Which ... was a neighbour to the man who fell into the hands of robbers? ... The one who had mercy on him ... Go and do likewise' (Luke 10:36,37).

'sinner'. Zacchaeus had probably never known such warmth before and his heart was melted. Without any challenge from Jesus about his dubious wealth, he stood up and declared, 'Here and now I give half of my possessions to the poor, and if I have cheated anybody out of anything, I will pay back four times the amount' (Luke 19:8).

These words and resultant actions showed that Zacchaeus had entered into the economy of God. He was no longer trusting in his riches. He'd seen Jesus and was convinced that he could live for something far better than mammon. Salvation came to him, his heart was touched and he gave.

The church should be renowned for its kindness and liberality. Jesus sacrificed His life for us. An appropriate reaction isn't, 'What blessings can I get out of God?' but 'What can I give to express my love and gratitude to Him?' One of the signs of spiritual maturity is seen in a heart of mercy towards the poor and a growth in practical generosity. If you look at the way you live, you should be able to determine if you're 'walking away sad' or whole-heartedly embracing the economy of God.

▓ Food for thought

➤ Read Ezekiel 16:48–50.

➤ What was the fate of Sodom?

➤ What does this verse tell you about how God views ministry to the poor?

➤ How does this challenge you?

▓ To consider

Consider Jesus' example to us; read 2 Corinthians 8:9 and Philippians 2:6–8.

List all that Jesus gave up for us.

_____

_____

_____

The Church of Jesus Christ is the most universal body in the world today. All we need to do is truly obey the one we rightly worship. But to obey will mean to follow. And he lives among the poor and oppressed, seeking justice for those in agony.
Ronald J. Sider

Here and now I give

All the believers were together and had everything in common. Selling their possessions and goods, they gave to anyone as he had need (Acts 2:42–44).

No-one claimed that any of his possessions was his own, but they shared everything they had ... There were no needy persons among them. For from time to time those who owned lands or houses sold them, brought the money from the sales and put it at the apostles' feet, and it was distributed to anyone as he had need (Acts 4:32,34,35).

The early church caught the spirit of Zacchaeus. Just as he had 'stood up and said to the Lord, "Look, Lord! Here and now I give ..."' (Luke 19:8), so they declared in action that they were reaching out to others.

They weren't communists whose focus was merely social good. They were people who were motivated by love for God. He had saved them and blessed them and now He was stirring them into action. It's possible that the likelihood of persecution stimulated many of them to sell their holdings and bless others in a remarkable way.

In Acts 6 we read about a problem regarding the distribution of food. The Hebraic widows who had extended families in the area, were receiving support from them which was over and above the daily food allowance. The Grecian widows who had travelled with their families and maybe returned to Jerusalem alone, didn't have any relatives who could help them and were struggling to make ends meet.

When the apostles heard about the problem, they didn't ignore it. They told the disciples to choose seven men who would be responsible for the food distribution. The consequence of this

▓ To do

List any skills or abilities you have which you could use to help the poor.

Do something practical to help someone in need this week, e.g. DIY, baking, help to fill out claim forms, etc.

▓ To meditate on

We must give ourselves to others.
'We have spoken freely to you ... and opened wide our hearts to you. We are not withholding our affection from you, but you are withholding yours from us. As a fair exchange ... open wide your hearts also' (2 Cor. 6:11–13).
'We loved you so much that we were delighted to share with you not only the gospel of God but our lives as well, because you had become so dear to us' (1 Thess. 2:8).

good administrative decision with regard to the needy was that the church continued to grow. So the daily care of the poor was clearly a characteristic of New Testament church life.

Some churches have, for years, been actively involved in caring for the poor. They've worked out programmes and have teams ministering in homes and on the streets. Individuals too have taken up the challenge. Some of the most generous people that I know don't have much in the way of the world's resources, but they give whatever they can.

Their hearts mirror the heart of God. For them, 'helping the poor' isn't just about 'writing another cheque'. It's about giving themselves. They bake cakes and share them, or repair equipment, or mow lawns, or decorate homes. The amazing thing is that many of them have major needs of their own — but the additional pressures bring out the sweetness in them.

Maybe you say, 'But I don't have the time or the energy.' Well I believe that you reap what you sow. If you plant beans, you'll get a harvest of beans. So if you don't have much time or energy, plant what little you do have and God will give them back to you.

➢ Read 2 Corinthians 9:6–15.

➢ Using a notebook rewrite this passage in your own words using analogies which are relevant to your situation.

➢ What is this passage saying to you?

▓ To discover

Find out if there are any widows or single parents in your church.

What is the church doing to support them?

What can you do to help?

Make a commitment to pray regularly for them that their needs will be met.

Much Christian preaching is genuinely beautiful. It speaks of a new force in human affairs, the self-giving love of God who became a poor man and gave his life for undeserving enemies. God's kingdom brings this pattern for relationships into men's lives.
Christopher Sugden

Sow and you'll reap

Blessed is he who has regard for the weak; the LORD delivers him in times of trouble. The LORD will protect him and preserve his life; he will bless him in the land and not surrender him to the desire of his foes. The LORD will sustain him on his sick-bed and restore him from his bed of illness (Ps. 41:1–3).

Honour the LORD with your wealth, with the firstfruits of all your crops; then your barns will be filled to overflowing, and your vats will brim over with new wine (Prov. 3:9,10).

W hen we reach out to the poor, we might think, 'I really don't know if God sees my work. And even if He does, I don't expect Him to do anything about it.' But the fact is that God is not only aware of our kindness to the needy, He promises to bless us for it.

David says that if we reach out to the weak, God will help us when we're weak (Ps. 41:1–3). The liberality that we show to the poor will return to us. In a sense, all believers, generous or otherwise, will know God's deliverance from difficulties. But He clearly has such a deep compassion for the weak, that those who help them will receive particular attention from Him.

Proverbs 14:31 says, 'He who oppresses the poor shows contempt for their Maker, but whoever is kind to the needy honours God.' The idea that our actions for others affect God is also reflected in Proverbs 19:17 — which, incidentally, is one of my favourite verses. 'He who is kind to the poor lends to the LORD, and he will reward him for what he has done.' You give to the needy; God effectively receives your gift and rewards you.

Again, we read, 'He who gives to the poor will lack nothing, but he who closes his eyes to

▓ To challenge

Look up 2 Corinthians 9:6 and Galatians 6:7,8.

What is the principle here?

_____

_____

What implication does it have for you?

_____

▓ To meditate on

Those who love the poor will be blessed. 'Good will come to him who is generous and lends freely, who conducts his affairs with justice ... He has scattered abroad his gifts to the poor ... his horn will be lifted high in honour' (Ps. 112:5,9).
'A generous man will prosper; he who refreshes others will himself be refreshed' (Prov. 11:25).
'Blessed is he who is kind to the needy' (Prov. 14:21).

them receives many curses' (Prov. 28:27). Here we have the economy of God and the economy of the world standing side by side. The Lord is over them both announcing that there's a law of return built into His Kingdom. One way leads to a blessing, the other to a curse.

The world says, 'You're foolish to give to the poor. Hold back!' God says, 'You're foolish to hold back. Give to the poor!' Which are you going to believe? Are you confident enough in God's Word to trust that what it says is the truth — however insane it may appear?

Farming is insane. Picture a new farmer. He borrows a big sum of money to rent land and equipment. Then he sows the seed and waits for a crop. 'I've never done this before,' he thinks, 'but the books and other farmers tell me it works. I'll just have to trust them.' For a long time he can't see any results, but then the harvest comes and he rejoices.

It starts with a risk. You hear from the Book and other Christians that God will bless you if you reach out to the poor. So you give — and what happens? You reap an abundant harvest. Then you realise from your own experience that what God says is 100% true.

▓ Food for thought

➤ Look up the following references: Proverbs 14:21; 21:13; 22:9,16,22,23; 28:27; 29:14; Ezekiel 16:49,50; Amos 2:6,7; Zechariah 7:8–14.

➤ What kind of people are blessed/cursed?

▓ To identify

Identify as many different ways as you can of honouring the Lord with your wealth.

_____

_____

_____

Which of these are you doing?

_____

Do you want to prove that God exists? Do you want to prove that God is alive and well? Do you want to prove that God still does things? Honour Him with your substance and you will see Him work in a manner that will exceed your greatest expectations.
R. T. Kendall

Justice and justice alone

'Do not use dishonest standards ... Use honest scales and honest weights'
(Lev. 19:35,36).

Do not have two differing weights in your bag — one heavy, one light. Do not have two differing measures in your house — one large, one small. You must have accurate and honest weights and measures
(Deut. 25:13–15).

Appoint judges and officials ... in every town ... and they shall judge the people fairly. Do not pervert justice or show partiality. Do not accept a bribe, for a bribe blinds the eyes of the wise and twists the words of the righteous. Follow justice and justice alone
(Deut. 16:18–20).

I n this study and the next I want to focus on some Old Testament teaching that will enhance our understanding of the way that the Jews regarded the matters of justice and righteousness.

First, I want to look at the principle that God's people should act justly in all their business transactions. This is emphasised in Leviticus 19:35,36 and Deuteronomy 25:13–15. The Jews used weights in the trading of goods. If they had two differing weights, they could actually make something appear heavier or lighter than it actually was. It was this kind of cheating that God wanted to prevent.

Society says, 'Rake in as much as you can and don't worry too much about others,' but God says, 'Look at every business transaction from both sides of the table.' If we're operating solely in our own interests, God will accuse us of using 'dishonest standards'. Our goal is to give the other person the better part of the deal. If we seek to do this, God will take pleasure in our work and bless us. We'll never come out the losers.

A second point I want to make is that in Israel, justice was demanded in the courts. God

▓ To read

Read Exodus 23:1–9.

Review your own lifestyle — do you act with justice in every area of your life?

What would a non-Christian colleague/friend/relative say about your standards of justice?

_____

_____

▓ To meditate on

God loves justice.
'Blessed are they who maintain justice, who constantly do what is right'
(Ps. 106:3).
'To do what is right and just is more acceptable to the LORD than sacrifice'
(Prov. 21:3).
'Act justly ... love mercy ... walk humbly with your God' (Mic. 6:8).
'So in everything, do to others what you would have them do to you'
(Matt. 7:12).

was concerned for the rights of everyone: the rich and influential, the poor and needy, the citizen and the sojourner. This protection is mentioned in Deuteronomy 16:18–20, but it also appears in several other places in the Scriptures.

God looks for a similar justice among us today. He wants to see leaders judging righteously in our nation and in our churches. And He watches to see whether we deal fairly with others. Do we in any way 'pervert justice or show partiality'? Do we favour a relative above a stranger? Do we shun the company of the lowly so that we can be seen chatting to the rich or famous? Do we judge people by their looks, their intelligence, or their job?

We may not be offering people 'bribes' as such, but in a quest for position or recognition, we might find ourselves doing all the outwardly acceptable things. We might allow others to control the way we think, to 'bribe' us into acting against our consciences for the sake of personal gain.

'Follow justice and justice alone' (v. 20) God said. Imagine how society would be transformed if everyone lived by that!

➤ Read your local newspaper every day this week.

➤ Make a note of any stories about injustice.

➤ Begin to think of ways in which you personally or your church could work towards seeing justice established.

☷ To consider

Christians today are more concerned with individual sinful acts than with their participation in unjust social structures.

What is meant by 'unjust social structures'?

_____

Do you agree with the statement above (Christians today ...)? Give reasons.

_____

Justice requires an end to our accumulation. A new commitment to economic sharing and simplicity will both break our bondage to affluence and bring a vitality and integrity that most of our congregations have never experienced.
Jim Wallis

Vain worship

'Seek justice,
encourage the
oppressed. Defend the
cause of the fatherless,
plead the case of the
widow' (Isa. 1:17).

Religion that God our
Father accepts as pure
and faultless is this: to
look after orphans and
widows in their distress
(James 1:27).

'Let justice roll on like a
river, righteousness like
a never-failing stream!'
(Amos 5:24)

Another Old Testament teaching that I want to consider concerns the protection of the rights of others. God particularly wanted the Jews to reach out to three types of people: the oppressed, the fatherless and the widow. He calls the church to do the same. Justice for others is crucial if we want to maintain our relationship with Him.

If God dealt with us according to His justice, we'd all be in a sorry state. But He comes to us with mercy and grace, and has forgiven our sins and given us eternal life. In view of His mercy to us, we must extend mercy to others — especially to those who are often insignificant in the eyes of the world. We must pray for them and work hard to see that they get justice.

The prophet Amos was raised up to address great injustice among the Israelites. The people had turned to pagan gods — although they were giving the impression that they were remaining faithful to the Lord. Their hearts were full of sin, but they were continuing to hold their annual religious festivals and were actually looking forward to the 'day of the Lord'.

God wasn't impressed by their hollow devotion. In fact, it sickened Him. He was

▓ **To identify**

Who, apart from the widows, fatherless and orphans need help in society?

_____

_____

In what ways can you reach out to each of these groups?

_____

_____

▓ **To meditate on**

Jesus sees through outward show. 'These people honour me with their lips, but their hearts are far from me. They worship me in vain' (Matt. 15:8,9). 'You hypocrites! You give a tenth of your spices ... But you have neglected the more important matters of the law — justice, mercy and faithfulness ... on the outside you appear to people as righteous but on the inside you are full of hypocrisy and wickedness' (Matt. 23:23,28).

looking for righteousness in their dealings with others. He wanted to see them demonstrating a proper fear of Him by upholding the cause of the poor. But they were exploiting the needy as if there were no God at all. They didn't have a proper relationship with the Lord, so they didn't treat others fairly. As far as God was concerned, their celebrations and sacrifices were useless because their lives weren't right.

Some Christians practise injustice during the week and join others to sing God's praises on Sundays. Their hearts are full of bitterness and anger. They steal, lie and cheat and then expect God to accept their worship and gifts. They fail to realise that when they're unjust towards their fellow human beings, they cut themselves off from God and render their devotion meaningless.

God's heart is for justice and righteousness, not outward show. The Israelites had turned religion into a ritual and Amos told them that the Lord would judge them for their hypocrisy. There is no way in which we can look forward to the coming of Jesus — the day of the Lord — unless our hearts are right; unless we're practising justice and righteousness every day.

> ➤ Read through the book of Amos, making notes as you go on the sort of sins God pinpointed in the people.

> ➤ Is God pinpointing any sin in your life? If so, put it right with Him.

▓ To acknowledge

How different are you on Sundays from the rest of the week?

What changes in your behaviour/attitudes need to take place for you to be consistent all the time?

_____

_____

_____

The biggest disease today is not leprosy or tuberculosis, but the feeling of being unwanted, uncared for and deserted by everybody. Our greatest problem is not hunger, but loneliness. The lack of love, the terrible indifference towards our neighbour who lives at the roadside assaulted by exploitation, corruption, poverty and disease.
Mother Teresa

Grant me justice

Then Jesus told his disciples a parable to show them that they should always pray and not give up. He said: 'In a certain town there was a judge who neither feared God nor cared about men. And there was a widow in that town who kept coming to him with the plea, "Grant me justice against my adversary"' (Luke 18:1–3).

Parables are word pictures which dramatise a truth. Jesus used them to communicate more effectively what He wanted to say. In Luke 18 we encounter a parable whose overall goal is to make us persistent in prayer. Prayer should be a constant reality for every believer.

This truth is underlined elsewhere in the Bible. Paul says that the 'weapons we fight with are not the weapons of the world' (2 Cor. 10:4). And when he writes to the Ephesians, he places prayer in the context of warfare (Eph. 6:18–20). 'Always keep on praying,' he says (Eph. 6:18), echoing Jesus' exhortation 'always pray and not give up' just before the story of the widow and the unjust judge.

As I look around, I'm delighted to see how seriously Christians are taking the need to spend time with God. Most people at the Vineyard pray and read their Bibles every day — some even several times a day. It blesses me to see them taking Scripture seriously and believing that things will be changed when they call on God for His help.

In this parable Jesus' teaching about prayer is in the context of justice. The Old and New Testament understanding of justice includes

▓ To pray

Spend time praying along the lines of 'Your kingdom come' (i.e. ask God to establish righteousness in unjust situations, to reign over puzzling circumstances, etc.).

Particularly ask the Lord for those in authority and for the government to bring justice to our nation.

▓ To meditate on

God's throne is built on justice. 'A sceptre of justice will be the sceptre of your kingdom' (Ps. 45:6). 'Righteousness and justice are the foundation of your throne' (Ps. 89:14). 'He will reign on David's throne and over his kingdom, establishing and upholding it with justice and righteousness ... for ever' (Isa. 9:7). 'I will make justice the measuring line and righteousness the plumb-line' (Isa. 28:17).

➤ Meditate on God's justice in Psalm 9.

he need for righteousness. So when we cry out for one, we automatically include the other. Jesus wants to establish His Kingdom on justice and righteousness, so He calls us to measure situations against the plumb-line of His righteousness and to pray that His Kingdom will come into any unjust situation — whether ours or that of someone else. Our constant cry, 'Your kingdom come!' will stir Him to bring things back into line with His will.

The judge in the story had no fear of God and cared nothing for men. Now the Jews of Jesus' day were always aware of God when they interacted with one another. The apostle John reflects this truth when he says that we can't love God and hate our brother at the same time (1 John 4:20). There wouldn't be any justice in that kind of relationship.

So as Jesus told this parable, His hearers would have thought that this judge was in big trouble because of his attitude towards God and man. They would also have realised that the widow who was coming to him could hardly expect to receive justice from someone who himself was obviously indifferent towards what was right and what was wrong.

▓ To assess

Are you indifferent to what is right and what is wrong? If not, what are you doing about it?

It is easy to think that we care, but care should be demonstrated by action.

Let us confine ourselves to the chief thought: prayer as an appeal to the friendship of God; and we shall find that two lessons are specially suggested. The one, that if we are God's friends, and come as such to Him, we must prove ourselves the friends of the needy; God's friendship to us and ours to others go hand in hand. The other, that when we come thus we may use the utmost liberty in claiming an answer.
Andrew Murray
With Christ in the School of Prayer

Press through

'Grant me justice against my adversary.' For some time he refused. But finally he said to himself, 'Even though I don't fear God or care about men, yet because this widow keeps bothering me, I will see that she gets justice, so that she won't eventually wear me out with her coming!' And the Lord said, 'Listen to what the unjust judge says. And will not God bring about justice for his chosen ones, who cry out to him day and night? Will he keep putting them off? I tell you, he will see that they get justice, and quickly. However, when the Son of Man comes, will he find faith on the earth?' (Luke 18:3–8)

The fact that the judge was indifferent to God and man didn't bother the widow. He was the only person available who had the power to grant her justice and she was going to get it from him. So she began pushing and pressing him for his intervention.

After a while, the judge decided that if he did nothing, the widow would 'wear (him) out'. The Greek word here gives the sense of being hounded, bombarded, beaten and given a black eye. This woman was so intolerably annoying that the judge couldn't stand it any more. Although he didn't care whether she got justice or not, he would give her what she wanted — just to get some peace and quiet.

Things are often accomplished by the sheer volume of persistent action. When you feel strongly enough about something, you can do a lot to make your point and get it changed. On an earthly plane, you can use your vote, write letters to local politicians or newspapers, support good causes, sign petitions, put up posters in your window, and, if necessary, resign from your job.

But the main emphasis of the parable is not so much on action as prayer. Jesus says that if

▓ To do

Write a letter to your MP about the government's policy towards the homeless, mentally ill or low paid, etc.

Be prepared to persist and to follow up any replies you may receive.

▓ To meditate on

The Lord will establish justice.
'He will make your righteousness shine like the dawn, the justice of your cause like the noonday sun' (Ps. 37:6).
'The LORD works righteousness and justice for all the oppressed' (Ps. 103:6).
'I know that the LORD secures justice for the poor and upholds the cause of the needy' (Ps. 140:12).
'My righteousness draws near speedily ... my arm will bring justice to the nations' (Isa. 51:5).

an unjust earthly judge can be persuaded to respond, how much more will a righteous divine Judge grant us justice if we pray 'day and night'. The One who has established His throne on righteousness and justice must eventually answer our consistent appeal to see His will done on earth as it is in heaven.

God will come against injustice — but in His time. 'With the Lord a day is like a thousand years' (2 Pet. 3:8). We aren't meant to predict when He will answer us; we're meant to pray. The apostle John implies that the prayers of the saints are stored, not lost (Rev. 8:3,4). We pray and God records everything we say. Then suddenly, one day He declares, 'Now I'll step in. Now they'll see that I've been listening. Now I'll bring justice and vindicate my name.'

There's another application to this parable too. If justice doesn't appear in our lifetime, it will come when Jesus returns to judge the nations. On that day He will lift oppression and straighten out all the injustices that have occurred throughout history. When He returns will He find us discouraged by our trials and full of despair, or fervent in prayer and abounding in faith?

▓ Food for thought

➤ Review Luke 18:1–8.

a) Why did the woman keep coming to the judge?

b) What do you think motivated her to carry on?

c) What was the result?

d) What does this tell us about God?

➤ Do you persist in prayer? If not, why not?

➤ Take one issue of injustice and make it your goal to persist in prayer about it until your prayer is answered.

▓ To consider

Given the choice would you prefer action for the poor to prayer about the poor? Give reasons.

_____

_____

Is either more important?

_____

Read Ephesians 6:12.
How does this verse affect your reasoning?

_____

Persevere; you do not know how near you are to the blessing you have sought for years.
F.B. Meyer

Against the tide

'You have heard that it was said, "Eye for eye, and tooth for tooth." But I tell you, Do not resist an evil person' (Matt. 5:38,39).

'You have heard that it was said, "Love your neighbour and hate your enemy." But I tell you: Love your enemies and pray for those who persecute you, that you may be sons of your Father in heaven' (Matt. 6:43–45).

Many years ago I was led to the Lord by someone who had been done a great injustice: a young man had abducted his daughter and killed her on a hillside. The grief-stricken father actually helped the police to find the offender and, while the prosecution was preparing its case, spoke to him about Jesus. The young man became a Christian, but he was found guilty of murder and was executed.

'I learnt to love him in Christ,' the father of the dead girl told me with tears in his eyes. 'But I could never touch him. I guess I just didn't love him enough.' It struck me that he loved 'his enemy' enough to tell him the good news about Jesus.

It's with great gratitude that I look back at my early Christian life. I was saved by a wonderful Lord and nurtured in a church where the leaders knew a lot about sacrificial living. They taught me by word and example about God's justice, and now the idea of justice and righteousness apart from Him is totally foreign to me.

I know that the solutions to the problems of mankind are not found in worldly forms of justice. It's no good our looking to politicians,

▓ To challenge

What kind of ambassador are you?

Seek God concerning any wrong attitudes that you may have towards others.

Come to God in repentance and ask for His righteousness and justice to come into your life.

▓ To meditate on

We must forgive.
'And when you stand praying if you hold anything against anyone, forgive him, so that your Father in heaven may forgive you your sins' (Mark 11:25).
'Jesus said, "Father, forgive them, for they do not know what they are doing"' (Luke 23:34).
'If you forgive anyone his sins, they are forgiven; if you do not forgive them, they are not forgiven' (John 20:23).

the police, the social services or the media for the answers. These organisations can go some way towards bringing justice, but they'll always fall short. So who will establish justice on earth (Isa. 42:4)? Only one person — Jesus.

We are His ambassadors. Wherever we go, we must take His justice. That means that we've got to allow Him to deal with any areas of unrighteousness in our own hearts. Do we hate others? Are we bigoted in our opinions? Do we readily take revenge when someone wrongs us? Do we revel in the downfall of others and the exaltation of ourselves? We must face and deal with these attitudes and act righteously towards everyone. Otherwise how can we bring justice to the nations?

All around us people are giving themselves to wickedness. God notices all injustice and calls us not only to be separate from it, but also to militate against it in prayer and action. Every time we cry out to Him; preach the gospel; hand out food and clothing; or lead someone to Christ, we're striking a blow against the tide of unrighteousness in our land. If you want a just society, you'll do all you can to proclaim Jesus and to demonstrate His love to others.

▓ To question

What would you have done if you'd been in the shoes of the bereaved man in the story?

_____

Why do people want to take revenge?

_____

Is it ever right to take revenge on another? Give reasons for your answer.

_____

▓ Food for thought

➤ Read Matthew 18:21–35.

➤ What lessons do you draw from this passage?

➤ How does it apply to you personally?

The church is only beginning to awaken to the reality that God expects his people to be advocates of justice, committed to ending oppression wherever it is found. And it is still hard for most Christians to realize that a major dimension of the mission of the church is to work for social justice by adopting more responsible lifestyles and becoming advocates of the poor in political and economic arenas.
Tom Sine

Jesus in disguise

'For I was hungry and you gave me something to eat, I was thirsty and you gave me something to drink, I was a stranger and you clothed me, I was sick and you looked after me, I was in prison and you came to visit me ... whatever you did for one of the least of these brothers of mine, you did for me' (Matt. 25:35,36,40).

Too often we distance ourselves from the needy. We know that Jesus wants us to reach out to them but we interpret this to mean taking some fruit to the harvest festival, donating a few old clothes to the Salvation Army, or sending a card to someone who's ill.

Now the elderly and the disabled may not be in a position to do more than this kind of thing and Jesus understands that and will reward them accordingly. But He's not impressed by able-bodied Christians who keep a respectable gap between themselves and the needy. On the Day of Judgement I can imagine His saying to them, 'For I was hungry, and you put some money in a tin and walked off.' He's looking for people who will roll up their sleeves and get involved — and that's something that many of us would rather leave to others.

Jesus calls us to feed the hungry and to clothe the naked. That doesn't mean tossing someone a sandwich and a bag of worn clothing. It means getting alongside him and demonstrating the compassion of God. At the Vineyard we have a huge warehouse of good secondhand clothing and people are actively engaged in feeding the hungry.

▓ To read

Read the story of the Good Samaritan (Luke 10:30–37).

What do you think was behind the behaviour of the Priest and the Levite?

_____

Do you recognise these attitudes in yourself, other Christians or your church?

▓ To meditate on

Jesus was compassionate to the needy. 'When Jesus landed and saw a large crowd, he had compassion on them and healed their sick' (Matt. 14:14). 'Jesus ... said, "I have compassion for these people; they have already been with me three days and have nothing to eat. I do not want to send them away hungry, or they may collapse on the way"' (Matt. 15:32).

Then there are the strangers. They may be foreigners or students who are feeling lonely because they're away from home. They may long to spend time with a family at the weekends but are rarely invited out. Perhaps we simply don't think about them. We have a warm home but it just doesn't cross our minds to share it with the strangers in our area.

What about the sick? It's interesting that Jesus didn't say, 'I was sick, and you healed me.' That doesn't mean that we stop praying for healing. On the contrary, Jesus has clearly commanded us to heal. So we pray for that, but if nothing happens we continue to reach out. Sometimes the most loving thing we can do is to spend time caring for someone who's ill.

Finally, there are the prisoners. I thank God for the development of the ministry to them. At the Vineyard we have several ex-prisoners who were converted as a direct result of the visits of church members. But there are also other 'prisoners' — the housebound. They'd love to have some company now and again.

Jesus is in disguise among us. He's looking for people who are willing to reach out to Him. Do you see Him? Are you helping?

▓ Food for thought

➤ Read Malachi 1:6–14.

➤ Consider the way in which you offer your sacrifices to God.

➤ What complaint might He make about you?

▓ To question

Circle the attitudes that have motivated you to help the poor in the past:

pity, embarrassment, compassion, bad conscience, desire to please God, seeing the need, following Jesus' example, duty.

Which is a right motivation? Support your answer from Scripture.

The contact of the affluent with the poor today is primarily through two means, television and statistics. We hear the stark statistics of human suffering and we watch starving children in living colour.
Jim Wallis

Do what the Father does

'I tell you the truth, the
Son can do nothing by
himself; he can do only
what he sees his Father
doing, because
whatever the Father
does the Son also does.
For the Father loves the
Son and shows him all
he does'
(John 5:19,20).

The church is called to be committed to the poor, but not all of us are required to serve them to the same degree. Jesus specifically told the rich young ruler and various others in church history to give up their possessions. He may ask you to do the same. Alternatively, He may want your main focus of attention to be on some other area of ministry.

The Holy Spirit equips God's people for individual tasks in the Kingdom. He calls some away from the pursuit of their careers and tells them to become involved in full-time Christian work. Then He moves others from one sort of employment to another. And He leaves a third group exactly where they are. Unless you hear from Him, you remain in your present situation and wait for His future direction.

Let's say that you don't feel God has called you to a ministry among the poor but that you are aware of your general responsibility to them. How do you react when you see a need? There's a drunk propped up against your garden wall and it's raining. Or there's a woman standing in the street asking you for money to catch a train. Should you respond every time you see a person in need? No.

▓ **To pray**

Pray for the gift of wisdom so that you can use your time and resources effectively.

▓ **To meditate on**

Everyone needs prudence.
'You who are simple, gain prudence' (Prov. 8:5).
'A simple man believes anything, but a prudent man gives thought to his steps ... The simple inherit folly, but the prudent are crowned with knowledge' (Prov. 14:15,18).
'A prudent man sees danger and takes refuge, but the simple keep going and suffer for it' (Prov. 22:3).

I believe that there were many needy people that Jesus never helped. He saw them in the towns that He visited but didn't stop for them. Why not? Because He did only what He saw the Father doing. If the Father told Him, 'Don't minister to that individual,' Jesus would obey.

We must learn to see the difference between the prompting of God and the pressing of a need — otherwise we'll spend our time with people whom the Lord hasn't sent to us.

At the Vineyard there is always a steady stream of individuals who want help. Many of them are real tricksters. 'I'm born again' they lie, and go on to share with us some cleverly-devised story that's designed to have us in tears. We do our best to avoid them.

Most of us are not good at noticing when God is at work and when He isn't. We must cultivate a greater sensitivity to the Holy Spirit. When we're faced with a need, we must pray, 'Father, have you sent this person? Do you want me to help him, or is he going to waste my time?' Sometimes, God will tell you to do nothing. Sometimes He may ask you to do more than you would have done. Develop the skill of listening and be ready to do whatever He says.

▓ Food for thought

➤ Set aside an hour to pray.

➤ Tell God how you feel about the issues you have covered so far in this study.

➤ Spend time listening for His response.

➤ Write down any clear direction He may give.

_____

_____

_____

_____

▓ To do

List as many qualities as you can of:

a good listener   a bad listener

_____   _____

_____   _____

_____   _____

_____   _____

Which list is most like you?

There is something very simple, almost childlike, about power evangelism. God gives impressions, and we act on them. If he does not speak to us, then we wait – something difficult for action-orientated Western people to do.
John Wimber

Make them come in

'The owner of the house became angry and ordered his servant, "Go out quickly into the streets and alleys of the town and bring in the poor, the crippled, the blind and the lame." "Sir," the servant said, "what you ordered has been done, but there is still room." Then the master told his servant, "Go out to the roads and country lanes and make them come in, so that my house will be full"' (Luke 14:21–23).

J esus once told a parable about a man who prepared a great banquet and then sent his servant to fetch those he'd invited. The servant met not with enthusiasm, but with excuses.

Although the would-be guests sounded sincere, they'd made other arrangements and simply didn't want to come. When the servant reported back, the master was angry and told him to go to the people who were hungry for answers to their blatantly obvious problems.

Sometimes we waste too much time on people who don't need or care about Jesus. We present the gospel to them, and they just make casual and superficial comments. 'Well,' they say indifferently, 'that's just your point of view. There are many ways to God. I just happen to believe in reincarnation. Besides, I've got a fabulous house, three cars and four televisions. I don't really need religion.'

Jesus calls us to reach the people who know that they have a need and who are desperate for help. 'Go out and make them come in,' He tells us. Although the poor, the crippled, the blind and the lame might recognise their needs, they might not initially accept the invitation. But we must persist in explaining it to them.

▓ To determine

Name three Bible characters who apparently refused Jesus' offer of eternal life and note what made them stumble.

_____

_____

_____

▓ To meditate on

Be enthusiastic about preaching Christ. 'Preach the good news to all creation' (Mark 16:15).
'We cannot help speaking about what we have seen and heard' (Acts 4:20).
'Those who had been scattered preached the word wherever they went' (Acts 8:4).
'Paul entered the synagogue and spoke boldly there ... arguing persuasively about the kingdom of God' (Acts 19:8).

When I was a young Christian people asked me why I was so effective at soul winning. I replied, 'I just get in their way. I tell them the good news until they stop letting me tell them. Then I go on telling them until they run away from me! Then I tell them again!'

Christians say to me, 'This person just won't listen to me any more and I want to maintain some sort of relationship or I'll lose him.' I reply, 'Well you've already lost him, so you may as well keep talking! At least he'll know he's fighting something. But if you become silent and he dies, how will you feel then?'

You've been given the privilege of inviting people to God's party and you must go first to those who have a need and know it. How do you identify them? You just start talking and sooner or later you're bound to see the sadness written on their faces and in their hearts.

Tell them that life extends beyond the grave. Tell them that they don't have to die helpless, broken and without hope. Tell them how they can find freedom through the atoning death of Christ. Compel them to come in! All that stands between them and the banquet is you and me — so get the invitations out!

▓ Food for thought

➤ Read Matthew 7:6; 10:14; Acts 13:44–52; 19:8–10.

➤ We are bound to face resistance to the gospel message but at what point should we shake the dust from our feet?

▓ To list

List the Scriptures you would use to point someone to Christ and keep the list in your wallet/handbag.

_____

_____

_____

It must never be forgotten that the enterprise required of us in evangelism is the enterprise of love: an enterprise that springs from a genuine interest in those whom we seek to win, and a genuine care for their well-being, and expresses itself in a genuine respect for them and a genuine friendliness towards them.
J. I. Packer

Ample resources available

God ... has blessed us in the heavenly realms with every spiritual blessing in Christ (Eph. 1:3).

God raised us up with Christ and seated us with him in the heavenly realms in Christ Jesus (Eph. 2:6).

We are God's workmanship, created in Christ Jesus to do good works, which God prepared in advance for us to do (Eph. 2:10).

Ministry is about meeting the needs of others on the basis of God's resources. But how can we sustain a ministry among the poor without becoming puffed up with pride or overcome with exhaustion? I believe that the answer is to know who we are in Christ — and much of that information is found in Paul's letter to the Ephesians.

Paul doesn't say that we've been given a 'few' or a 'lot of' spiritual blessings. He says that we've been given 'every spiritual blessing in Christ'. Each one of us has all the resources of heaven to meet any challenge and to fulfil any ministry that God gives to us.

It's hard to understand how we can be living on earth and yet at the same time be 'seated in heavenly places'. Perhaps an athletic analogy will help. Let's say we enter a marathon and are told by the organisers, 'You're being awarded the first place trophy before you run the race.' That's what it's like to have victory in Christ before we go out and minister.

The analogy doesn't stop there because we must still run the race. So imagine that the organisers then give us a special concoction and say, 'Right, drink this. It will give you

▨ To ask

What resources do you need from God?

_____

_____

_____

Ask for and receive His blessing.

▨ To meditate on

We have complete victory in Christ.
'We are more than conquerors through him who loved us' (Rom. 8:37).
'He gives us the victory through our Lord Jesus Christ' (1 Cor. 15:57).
'God ... always leads us in triumphal procession in Christ' (2 Cor. 2:14).
'Everyone born of God overcomes the world. This is the victory that has overcome the world, even our faith' (1 John 5:4).

unlimited strength and speed. When you run, you won't lose — and besides, you've already got the trophy.' That's how our position in Christ affects our ministry: we're in a race that we've already won, and while we minister we have all the riches of heaven at our disposal.

God's salvation is given with a purpose: to do good works. When we become Christians Jesus effectively tells us, 'Right, now that your future is secure you can start doing the things that my Father has prepared for you.'

The real test of spiritual maturity is not the ability to speak in tongues, prophesy, or memorise Scripture. It's the ability to serve God and others through good works. We fulfil our purpose on earth by learning to love and serve the unlovely, the downtrodden and the less fortunate.

If we don't know who we are in Christ, we'll find ourselves reaching out to the needy in our own strength and will collapse under the great weight of pressure. But if we recognise that we've been blessed with all the resources of heaven and given complete victory in Christ, we will always have the love to share with them and the power to change their lives.

▓ Food for thought

➤ Read through Ephesians 1 and 2.

➤ Particularly note the phrases 'in Him' and 'in Christ'.

➤ Write out your own explanation of what it means to be 'in Christ'.

_____

_____

_____

_____

▓ To list

List any good works you have performed for others in the last seven days.

_____

_____

Now list some that you could do during the next seven days.

_____

_____

Many live under obedience more of necessity than of love, and such people are often discontented and complaining. They will never attain freedom of mind unless they submit with their whole heart for the love of God.
Thomas à Kempis

Servant or lord?

'The kings of the
Gentiles lord it over
them ... But you are not
to be like that. Instead,
the greatest among
you should be like the
youngest, and the one
who rules like the one
who serves ... I am
among you as one who
serves' (Luke 22:25–27).

J esus didn't lord it over people; He served them — and He told us to do the same. Sadly, we sometimes forget that we're His servants and become self-centred. 'The church is here to serve me,' we think, and we make all sorts of demands on others. Jesus wants us to return to His original plan for us. It's only when we're serving that we'll truly be fulfilled.

Jackie Pullinger-To is the sort of person who jolts us out of our self-centredness and plunges us into the reality of service. For a number of years she's been ministering to the poor on the streets of Hong Kong. Many of those she helps are drug addicts or prostitutes — but she reaches out to all of them with the love and compassion of Jesus.

God has blessed her work. Many people have been saved and are now ministering alongside her in houses that she's set up to cater for the needy. Christians write to her from all over the world offering long- or short-term help, and many go out and return with a fresh passion in their hearts to reach the poor.

Once, when Jackie was in America, I talked to her about our sending a few members of the Vineyard to Hong Kong every three or four

▓ To pray

Pray for Jackie Pullinger-To and her workers.

Pray also for any particular individuals who are serving God in difficult situations.

▓ To meditate on

Servants must serve.
'Whoever wants to become great among you must be your servant, and whoever wants to be first must be slave of all' (Mark 10:43,44).
'So you also, when you have done everything you were told to do, should say, "We are unworthy servants; we have only done our duty"' (Luke 17:10).
'Serve wholeheartedly, as if you were serving the Lord, not men' (Eph. 6:7).

months. She answered, 'Do you realise what they'd be committing themselves to?' Well I hadn't the slightest idea, so she told me.

'They'd have to work from fifteen to eighteen hours a day,' she said. 'And that's every day. There'd be no breaks — no opportunities to get away from people — they'd just be on duty all the time. And they'd have to be ready to step in if a couple of the boys came at each other with knives — which is sometimes what happens.'

'What sort of work do you want them to do?' I asked her. 'How about teaching?' 'If they can speak any of the three Chinese dialects, yes,' she replied. 'But what we're really looking for are individuals who will scrub floors, clean toilets, cook food and make beds.' Then she added, 'You know, few people want to do these things for eighteen hours a day, seven days a week. But that's what we need.'

If we're chasing after personal recognition, we'll never humble ourselves to do menial tasks. If our goal is to serve, we'll jump at any opportunity to bless others — particularly those who can't help themselves. Look at your contribution to church life and ask yourself, 'In practice, am I a servant or a lord?'

▓ Food for thought

➤ Read John 13:1–17.

➤ What are the characteristics of a servant?

➤ How do you measure up?

▓ To question

Read Luke 16:10–12.

Are you prepared to do anything for God, however trivial or mundane?

No one wanted to be considered the least. Then Jesus took a towel and a basin and so redefined greatness. Having lived out servanthood before them (the disciples) He called them to the way of service.
Richard Foster

Take the lowest place

'When you are invited, take the lowest place, so that when your host comes, he will say to you, "Friend, move up to a better place." Then you will be honoured in the presence of all your fellow guests. For everyone who exalts himself will be humbled, and he who humbles himself will be exalted' (Luke 14:10,11).

It's a basic principle in the Kingdom — that if we exalt ourselves, God will humble us. He knows that if we start thinking how wonderful we are, we will damage His work — so He steps in to prevent this from happening.

Many of us have learnt a little about the importance of serving without drawing attention to ourselves. We know something about giving secretly to others and about helping the poor. But then the enemy creeps in and tries to trip us into adopting a haughty attitude concerning what we're doing.

This happened at the Vineyard several years ago. We were reaching out to others and God was really blessing our ministry among the sick. In fact, our reputation for healing went round the world. We praised God for the power He was releasing among us, but then some of our team members began to fall into pride. We had to address this and encourage them simply to be grateful that God was using them.

Some Christians don't mind being humble for a while — so long as they can get what they want. That's not the right attitude. It reflects a preoccupation with worldly reward — the desire to be exalted only in the eyes of people.

▒ To pray

Pray for those in authority in your local church, asking for God's blessing on their ministry.

▒ To meditate on

God responds to the humble.
'You save the humble' (Ps. 18:27).
'He guides the humble in what is right and teaches them his way' (Ps. 25:9).
'The LORD sustains the humble' (Ps. 147:6).
'The LORD ... crowns the humble with salvation' (Ps. 149:4).
'God ... gives grace to the humble' (James 4:6).

God will exalt the humble — but that may be on the last day when He commends us for being good and faithful servants (Matt. 25:23). It's legitimate to be motivated by this ultimate reward, but not by the sort of reward that appeals to the flesh, the one that honours you and subtly pushes God into the background.

Humility is seen both in action and attitude. It's our job to take the lowliest place at the banqueting table and to be willing to stay there or to be moved up as God directs. Maybe He will give us visibility; maybe He won't. That's His choice and we must be happy with it.

One day perhaps God will ask you to take on a more prominent role. You may find yourself involved in some significant ministry. But if you're humble, you won't assume that you'll be there for ever. After a while, God may say, 'That's enough. I've decided to exalt someone else now. So you go back where you were.'

If you're wise, you won't try to continue the work you've been doing. You'll hurry back down to the foot of the table, rejoicing that you've played your part and praying fervently that God will bless the person who'll be taking over from you.

➤ Using Luke 22:25–27 as a starting point, contrast the words Jesus uses to define greatness with those the world chooses.

▓ To consider

Think about John the Baptist's statement 'He must become greater; I must become less' (John 3:30).

What is this verse saying to you?

_____

_____

_____

A Christian is a perfectly free lord of all, subject to none. A Christian is a perfectly dutiful servant of all, subject to all.
Martin Luther

Trust, do, dwell and enjoy

Trust in the LORD and do good; dwell in the land and enjoy safe pasture (Ps. 37:3).

I love Psalm 37 because it contains so many great promises for those who trust God and do good. Please find it in your Bible because I want to look at some of the verses in it.

We'll start with verse 3 which tells us that there's a link between trusting, doing, dwelling and enjoying. If we seek a relationship with God and engage in good deeds, God will establish and bless us.

In verses 18 and 19 we're told that the blameless are known to God. He promises that they will enjoy plenty while others are experiencing famine. Our definition of 'plenty' may not coincide with God's, but it's clear that we'll have an ample supply to meet our needs. This is a really encouraging word in the face of economic recession.

Going on to verse 22, we see God's mercy and justice working side by side. He blesses some and curses others. We are His children, the apple of His eye. We should look for God's blessing on our lives. We can't earn it, but we can do good because we're so grateful that His favour already rests on us.

Verses 25 and 26 are promises for righteous and generous people. Again, the emphasis is on

▓ To memorise

Read through Psalm 37.
Write out the verse which means the most to you.

_____

_____

_____

_____

Memorise this verse.

▓ To meditate on

God's promises have never failed.
'Not one of all the LORD's good promises to the house of Israel failed; every one was fulfilled' (Josh. 21:45).
'God ... has fulfilled what he promised ... to my father David' (1 Kings 8:15).
'What God promised our fathers he has fulfilled for us' (Acts 13:32,33).
'After waiting patiently, Abraham received what was promised' (Heb. 6:15).

trusting and doing which lead to blessing. When God sees a righteous life, He lavishes His love both on that person and on his children.

Finally verse 34 exhorts us to wait for God and to keep His way — because one day we'll be exalted and the wicked will be humbled.

It's easy to become impatient and give up. We try to love others but the work's plain hard and often unrewarding. Then we glance round at people who seem to be getting away with murder and question, 'Doesn't God see that? Then why doesn't He do something about it?'

He will. The day of judgement will reveal to the whole world that God cannot be mocked. On that day, those who've rejected the way of salvation will be condemned, the works of lazy believers will be burnt up — although the people will be saved, and faithful Christians will receive God's 'well done'. Everyone will reap exactly as he or she has sown.

God is looking for people who will enjoy their relationship with Him, catch His heart of compassion for others, and reach out to them with expressions of practical concern. That's our calling. God's blessing rests on everyone who fulfils it.

▓ Food for thought

➤ Read 2 Peter 3.

➤ How does this passage challenge you specifically?

➤ List ways in which you can 'make every effort to be found spotless, blameless and at peace with him' (2 Pet. 3:14).

_____

_____

_____

_____

▓ To thank

List the ways in which God has been blessing you recently.

_____

_____

_____

_____

_____

Set aside time just to thank Him for these things.

God deals lovingly and gently with us. His desire is that everything be offered to Him, but He will not take everything away from us. All needs to be at His disposal, remembering always that it is His purpose to give. He only takes in order that He may measure back to us immeasurably more than we have given.
Colin Urquhart

Wanted: willing volunteers

Then I heard the voice of the Lord saying, 'Whom shall I send? And who will go for us?' And I said, 'Here am I. Send me!' (Isa. 6:8)

Never be lacking in zeal, but keep your spiritual fervour, serving the Lord' (Rom. 12:11).

L et me encourage you — don't wait for the local church to start reaching out to the needy before you do anything. Pray for a burden for the lost. Find out what God is doing and do it alongside Him. He will give you the opportunities to minister.

A number of years ago a young couple in the church were winning many people to Christ. Then the wife became pregnant. They went on with their evangelism for a while, but in the ninth month she really couldn't keep going out and meeting unbelievers. The trouble was that she had a deep passion to reach them.

One night she was talking to me about this and weeping. 'The doctor wants me to stay at home now,' she said. 'But I want to continue God's work. What can I do?' 'Well,' I replied, 'why don't we pray that He'll send people to your door?' So we prayed — and He did! Day after day He brought individuals to her. She witnessed to them and many of them became Christians. All God wanted was someone who was willing to be involved.

If you're willing, God will bring the right people to you. The problem often lies in the willingness. You consider opening your home to

▨ To review

Review your attitude to your possessions.

Are you willing to share them with *anyone*?

Think about your most treasured possession. What would your reaction be if were stolen/broken/defaced or similar?

▨ To meditate on

Cultivate a willingness to do things.
'Everyone who was willing ... brought an offering to the Lord' (Exod. 35:21).
'Grant me a willing spirit to sustain me' (Ps. 51:12).
'Your troops will be willing on your day of battle' (Ps. 110:3).
'Do not be proud, but be willing to associate with people of low position' (Rom. 12:16).
'Be generous and willing to share' (1 Tim. 6:18).

strangers and suddenly you're picturing the most distasteful combination of events that might happen. 'What about my sofa?' you think. 'Supposing someone vomits all over it! And what if they smoke cannabis, stub out their cigarettes on the furniture and toss them into the Ming vase?! Will they steal things? No, I really don't think I could cope.'

Maybe these sorts of things will happen, maybe they won't. Maybe the experience of reaching out to people will be one of the most significant landmarks in your life. Why? Because God is behind it. Some of the greatest blessings that I've ever had have come through packages that at first didn't excite me much. I've seen a needy person and have thought, 'This isn't a good deal!' But I've been wrong and God has moved in.

So don't be afraid of what the Lord might ask you to do. He'll give you the opportunities and the resources. Learn how to be generous with your life. If you started today just think how much you could do for others in a week, a year, or even ten years. God wants to establish His Kingdom among the poor. He's looking for volunteers. Is your hand in the air?

▧ Food for thought

➤ Refer back to your research about local charities/projects (Study 1).

➤ Volunteer to help in any way you can for one evening/weekend, e.g. help in soup kitchen, serve in charity shop, visit the elderly.

▧ To pray

Can you honestly say 'Here I am, send me' to the Lord?

Pray about anything you feel holds you back from volunteering freely.

Ask the Lord to set you free from any fears.

God has not asked us to be responsible for the problem of world hunger. Rather God has offered us the privilege of participating in the lives of others out of the wealth he has put in our care.
Tony Campolo & Gordon Aeschliman

Over to you

Jesus went through all the towns and villages, teaching in their synagogues, preaching the good news of the kingdom and healing every disease and sickness (Matt. 9:35).

'As the Father has sent me, I am sending you' (John 20:21).

Jesus had a plan for His disciples. First, He called them to Himself. Then He took them round with Him and showed them what He wanted them to do. Next He sent them out on their own. And finally He ascended and left them to carry on without His physical presence

The Twelve were with Jesus for about three years. Day by day they followed Him into the streets and watched the way that He related to people. They saw Him associating with the poor and needy and with the rich and influential. He proclaimed the gospel of the Kingdom wherever He went and He healed all kinds of diseases.

During the early days of Jesus' ministry, those disciples must have been completely overwhelmed by what was happening. There were crowds pressing in on them wherever they went, miracles going on all around them and increasing opposition from the religious leaders They must have been anxious for themselves, and amazed at the incredible impact that Jesus was having on the community. I wonder how they reacted when one day, the Lord said to them, 'Right, now it's your turn.'

Many Christians think that it's enough just to be numbered with Jesus, let alone act on His

▓ **To do**

Ask someone you know who has a ministry among the poor to disciple you, as you begin to reach out yourself.

▓ **To meditate on**

Remember the poor.
'Do not be afraid, little flock, for your Father has been pleased to give you the kingdom. Sell your possessions and give to the poor. Provide purses for yourselves that will not wear out, a treasure in heaven that will not be exhausted, where no thief comes near and no moth destroys. For where your treasure is, there your heart will be also' (Luke 12:32–34).